THE GEORGE
WASHINGTON
UNIVERSITY
LAW SCHOOL
WASHINGTON DC

MIPLC Studies

Volume 18

Joel Gotkin

The United States Bayh-Dole Act and its Effect on University Technology Transfer

MIPLC Munich Intellectual Property Law Center
Augsburg München Washington DC

Die Deutsche Nationalbibliothek verzeichnet diese Publikation in der Deutschen Nationalbibliografie; detaillierte bibliografische Daten sind im Internet über http://dnb.d-nb.de abrufbar.

The Deutsche Nationalbibliothek lists this publication in the Deutsche Nationalbibliografie; detailed bibliographic data is available in the Internet at http://dnb.d-nb.de .

a.t.: Washington DC, George Washington University, Juris Doctorate Degree, 2011 and Munich, Intellectual Property Law Center, Master Thesis (LL.M.), 2011

ISBN 978-3-8329-7706-1

1. Auflage 2012

Table of Contents

Abstract

This thesis undertakes to examine the effect of the United States Bayh-Dole Act on technology transfer, specifically with respect to universities. The Bayh-Dole Act was enacted in 1980 to promote utilization of inventions that arise from federally funded research and development. The United States Government had a renewed focus on research and development after World War II, and the Act undertook to maximize the public benefits of such R&D. This paper examines two components of the Act: the general shift in ownership away from the government, and the march-in provision that the government can use to assert certain rights in specific circumstances.

The thesis begins by surveying the technology transfer sector in the United States before and after the passing of the Act, and notes the historical shifts in tendencies and preferences on the part of the government that led Congress to pass the Bayh-Dole Act. The introductory portion of the paper also notes the trends in university patenting and portfolio management in the years leading up to Bayh-Dole, and proceeds by providing a brief overview of the legislative history of the Act. The second chapter of the paper examines specific provisions of the Act which will be analyzed in later chapters, notably the disposition of rights that includes the shift in ownership, as well as the march-in provision.

After a brief summary of perceived strengths and weaknesses of the Act, this paper will analyze one of the Act's most controversial components – the government's march-in provision. This provision allows for the government to require the contractor to license, or even grant a license itself, if the contractor is not achieving practical application, or the action is necessary for certain other policy reasons. The thesis will detail two petitions to the NIH requesting the agency to use its march-in rights to license a patent, and note that in these cases and every other case since the passing of the Act, the government has failed to utilize its march-in rights. The thesis will then derive the conclusion that a march-in provision is necessary in theory, but the provision as currently interpreted needs to be amended to ensure that the government does utilize its right to force a license when the need arises.

The second area of analysis focuses on the crux of the Bayh-Dole Act – the ability for a contractor to assert patent ownership. Prior to the Act, the government retained all rights to inventions created with any government funding, and the government's failure to commercialize its patent portfolio led to many underutilized patents and a general failure to provide the public with the fruits of the R&D. The Act has been examined by many academics to determine whether or not this "shift in ownership" has ultimately benefited the technology transfer system in the United States. This paper will present empirical analysis that acknowledges that while Bayh-Dole was surely not the only factor leading to a more dynamic, efficient, and successful commercial marketplace for university-created and federally funded inventions, it did have a significant effect on the system.

Specifically, the paper will examine the increase in patenting subsequent to Bayh-Dole, and determine the level that the statute itself was key to this increase. The paper will empirically examine the "quality" of the patents, in an effort to determine whether or not Bayh-Dole led to an increase in utility in addition to the increase in number. The paper will also look into the biotechnology field and assess its dependency on patenting and university research. The paper will note that the biotech field was particularly benefited by the Bayh-Dole Act, and explain how this reconciles with the fact that the rise in biotech patenting began slightly before the passing of the Act.

Critics of Bayh-Dole contend that early stage patenting by multiple inventors could lead to a license stacking problem as well as deter future R&D, which comprises an "anticommons" concern. The thesis will empirically examine the effect Bayh-Dole has had on commercialization, and conclude that the extreme success in this area negates the hypothesis that Bayh-Dole has contributed to such a problem. This portion of the paper will conclude by noting Bayh-Dole has neither hampered nor distorted research and scientific progress, despite the renewed focus on commercialization instead of research for pure academic pursuit.

After addressing the two main components of the Bayh-Dole Act, the paper will move to the future of the Act, beginning by assessing the Supreme Court decision in the recent *Stanford v. Roche* case. The *Stanford* case involved an invention developed by an employee of Stanford, who agreed to assign his rights to the university. However, the employee also assigned his rights to Cetus, a company that later sold its interests to Roche. The Supreme Court determined that the contract with Stanford involved only a future assignment of rights, while the contract with Cetus involved a present transfer of rights. Thus, Roche won the case on a contracting technicality.

Though the case was decided based partially on contract law, the implications of this case will be strong in the university technology transfer sector. First, the Supreme Court made it abundantly clear that Bayh-Dole does *not* trump the rights of an inventor to his invention. Thus, regardless of the Bayh-Dole Act, the true inventor of an invention keeps his ownership rights, absent any assignment or contract stating otherwise. If Bayh-Dole was interpreted to supersede this principle of patent law, Stanford would have won the case, and the implications for technology transfer could become dire if inventors became less willing to innovate because of the fact that a university employer would automatically gain ownership in their work.

Though the court likely decided the case correctly from a policy perspective, this decision will still affect the university technology transfer sector. First, universities will have to draft contracts more strictly and do more research to determine if an inventor has already assigned his rights to another party. This could lead to a more regimented, formal relationship between universities and employees, which could ultimately impair the commercialization of technology.

The case also brings to light a formal gap between the Bayh-Dole obligations and patent rights. The government expects to gain its rights to march-in and a nonexclusive license, which would come if the contractor elects to enforce its ownership. The holding in the case contemplates that an inventor may assign away his rights, leaving the contractor and by extension, the government, without any rights. This could complicate the front end of technology transfer, where the government may be less willing to engage in funding certain research.

Finally, the case creates the possibility that there will be multiple parties claiming ownership of certain parts of patentable inventions, most notably the inventor and any of his assignees, as well as the university. This could exacerbate the anticommons concern that is already very prevalent in patent law. Multiple owners are less incentivized to commercialize or further innovate if their ownership is shared.

The thesis ultimately views the Act from an international perspective, and notes specific countries that have utilized or attempted to legislate "Bayh-Dole-esque" provisions. Japan created a "Bayh-Dole Act" twelve years ago, and is starting to see improvements in its technology transfer sector, despite fundamental differences in both university structure and cultural preferences as compared to the United States. Numerous countries in the European Union, including Germany, have legislated similar provisions in an attempt to enhance their technology transfer sectors. One developing country in particular, India, has been wrestling with a Bayh-Dole Bill for several years. India has been hesitant to pass its bill because of stark differences between the economies, university systems, and overall patent culture between itself and the United States. An assessment of these three countries leads to the conclusion that Bayh-Dole provisions can have a successful performance abroad, provided countries narrowly tailor the law to ensure their particular technology transfer tendencies are incorporated and commercialization is maximized based on their own structures and principles.

Acronyms and Abbreviations

AIDS	Acquired Immune Deficiency Syndrome
AUTM	Association of University Technology Managers
BDA	Bayh-Dole Act
CAFC	Court of Appeals for the Federal Circuit
CIMIT	Center for Integration of Medicine and Innovative Technology
CFR	Code of Federal Regulations
CEU	Council of the European Union
CSIR	Council of Scientific and Industrial Research in India
DOD	Department of Defense
DOE	Department of Energy
EU	European Union
FDA	Food and Drug Administration (USA)
GAO	Government Accountability Office
HIV	Human Immunodeficiency Virus
IP	Intellectual Property
IPA	Institutional Patent Agreement
JHU	Johns Hopkins University
NACUA	National Association of College and University Attorneys
NASA	National Aeronautics and Space Administration
NIH	National Institutes of Health
R&D	Research and Development
SCOTUS	Supreme Court of the United States
UK	United Kingdom
U.S.	United States
USC	United States Code

I. Introduction

In 2005, Emory University concluded what is widely considered the largest known intellectual property deal involving an American university, receiving $525 million in exchange for the rights to an anti-HIV drug, Emtriva.[1] The drug was invented by three faculty members using federal government funding, yet Emory was able to attain ownership and sell the drug for profit. Emory was able to achieve this pursuant to the passing of the 1980 Patent and Trademark Law Amendments Act, which is colloquially referred to as the Bayh-Dole Act (hereinafter "BDA").[2]

Emory noted that its share of the transaction will be "reinvested in [its] research mission following the terms of the Bayh-Dole Act... to encourage commercialization of research by universities."[3] This statement echoes one of the main policy objectives of a statute that has been hailed by many as the "most inspired piece of legislation to be enacted in America over the past half-century"[4] and bemoaned by others as gaining undeserved attention and potentially counterproductive.[5]

This paper will describe the technology transfer system in the United States and present a brief history of the BDA. A detailed discussion of the Act and its most noteworthy provisions will follow. I will continue by discussing some perceived strengths and weaknesses of the statute, and proceed to analyze the true effect of the two most important aspects of the Act: the march-in provision and change in

1 *See* David Wahlberg, *Emory Gets $525 Million Payment for Emtriva,* ATL. J. CONST., July 19, 2005, *quoted in* HIVPlusmag.com, *available* at http://www.hivplusmag.com/NewsStory.asp?id=12287&sd=07/20/2005.

2 *See* Bayh-Dole Act, UD Research, University of Delaware, *available at* http://www.udel.edu/research/protecting/bayh-dole.html.The name "Bayh-Dole" Act originates from the sponsors of the bill in Congress – Senator Birch Bayh (D- Indiana) and Senator Robert Dole (R-Kansas). *See* Jennifer A. Henderson and John J. Smith, *Academia, Industry, and the Bayh-Dole Act: An Implied Duty to Commercialize,* paper supported in part by a grant from the Center for Integration of Medicine and Innovative Technology (CIMIT), at 3.

3 *See* Press Release, Gilead Sciences, Emory University and Royalty Pharma, GILEAD SCIENCES AND ROYALTY PHARMA ANNOUNCE $525 MILLION AGREEMENT WITH EMORY UNIVERSITY TO PURCHASE ROYALTY INTEREST FOR EMTRICITABINE (July 18, 2005), *available at* http://www.emory.edu/news/Releases/emtri.

4 *See Innovation's golden goose: The reforms that unleashed American innovation in the 1980s, and were emulated widely around the world, are under attack at home*, THE ECONOMIST, Dec 12, 2002. This article has been one of the most widely cited opinion pieces by Bayh-Dole supporters, as it attempts to explain how Bayh-Dole has brought America back to a "pre-eminent" technology powerhouse.

5 Bayh Dole's effects are not supported by "hard evidence." *See* DAVID C. MOWERY, ET AL., IVORY TOWER AND INDUSTRIAL INNOVATION: UNIVERSITY-INDUSTRY TECHNOLOGY TRANSFER BEFORE AND AFTER THE BAYH-DOLE ACT IN THE UNITED STATES 97 (Martin Kenney and Bruce Kogut eds., Stanford University Press) (2004).

presumption of ownership. Ultimately, I will present the recent *Stanford v. Roche* case as a potential limitation of the scope of the Act, and examine the effect Bayh-Dole has had in technology transfer systems of other countries.

While the BDA has been empirically proven to have a positive effect on United States technology transfer, the statute is not perfect; it contains a march-in provision that was created to help the government protect the public interest, but fails in practice. A limitation on the Bayh-Dole Act has been surfaced by the *Stanford* case, which may have a future effect on university technology transfer. Furthermore, though Bayh-Dole has proved successful in the United States, great care should be taken in using similar statutes abroad. The United States has a unique university structure and distinctive research, development and government funding methods. Thus, a statute regulating such transfer needs to be narrowly tailored to the preferences of the relevant country.

A. *Introduction to Technology Transfer*

Pursuant to the BDA, universities conducting research using government funds can elect to retain title to inventions that arose from those funds, so long as they satisfy certain requirements.[6] This "give and take" system introduced by the BDA has had a substantial influence on university technology transfer since 1980.

Technology transfer is the transfer of the assets related to a technology from one entity to another. In practice, this will often involve both the exchange of knowledge and information as well as the transfer of an intellectual property right.[7] The most general methods in which one can transfer these intangible assets are via the license contract or an assignment contract.[8]

6 *See* David M. Kettner and William J. Decker, *Fundamentals of Technology Transfer and Intellectual Property Licensing*, November 2004 NACUA CLE Workshop Outline, *reprinted in* Technology Transfer Issues for Colleges and Universities: A Legal Compendium (Judith L. Curry, ed., National Association of College and University Attorneys 2005). These requirements include filing patent applications and seeking commercialization of the invention.

7 *See id.* at 10.

8 While each term carries its own inherent complexities, the fundamental difference between a license and an assignment is that a license is a revocable contract where the licensor (party granting the license) retains ownership while the licensee (party receiving the license) is afforded the opportunity to "work" the right. In contrast, an assignment is an irrevocable agreement where ownership of the right is transferred permanently from the assignor (grantor) to assignee (grantee). *See* Phillip Mendes, *To License a Patent – or, to Assign it: Factors Influencing the Choice*, *published by* WIPO, *available at* http://wipo.int/export/sites/www/sme/en/documents/pdf/license_assign_patent.pdf.

1. Licenses and Assignments Used by Universities in Technology Transfer

Universities often pen assignment contracts between themselves and their employees to ensure that the universities gain the ownership of the invention. Thus, universities would be able to capitalize on inventions produced by their faculty. These assignments can be reflected in a general "patent policy"[9] or enacted upon signature of a patent transfer agreement.[10] The transfer of rights between the inventor and the funded institution has consequences with respect to ownership, which will be examined generally in Chapter III, *infra*, and specifically with respect to the *Stanford v. Roche* case in Chapter V, *infra.*

The BDA also compels universities to license inventions. First, the government retains a nonexclusive license to practice for or on behalf of the United States.[11] Secondly, universities grant licenses to commercial entities. Implicit in the BDA is that a university must attempt to commercialize its inventions, which in practice often involves a license to a third party in exchange for royalty payments.[12] Bayh-Dole effected license agreements between universities and licensees may be either exclusive or nonexclusive, and tend to mirror a typical patent license agreement.[13]

2. Prohibition on Assignments by Universities to Third Parties

While the BDA arguably imposes a duty on universities to commercialize, the Act constricts universities by eliminating the possibility of assignment in most situa-

9 *See* Research Policies: University of Delaware Office of the Executive Vice President and University Treasurer, *available at* http://www.udel.edu/ExecVP/policies/research/6-06.html. "it is the policy of the University that all inventions and discoveries,... which are conceived or reduced to practice or developed by University faculty, staff, or students in the course of employment at the University... shall be the property of the university." *Id.*

10 Stanford University requires all relevant personnel to sign a Patent and Copyright Agreement, which currently references its policy and states, in part, "I hereby assign to Stanford all my right, title and interest in such patentable inventions..." *See* Patent and Copyright Agreement for Stanford Personnel, Research Policy Handbook: Memo, *available at* http://rph.stanford.edu/su18.html. This policy has been clearly amended subsequent to a Supreme Court decision finding that Stanford's previous assignment was merely a future interest. *See* Board of Trustees of the Leland Stanford Junior University v. Roche Molecular Systems, Inc., et al., 563 U. S. ___ (2011) at page 8. This case and its effects on technology transfer will be discussed in chapter V, *infra.*

11 *See* 35 U.S.C. § 202(c)(4) (2009).

12 *See generally* 35 U.S.C. § 203(a)(1) (2009), explaining that the government can "march-in" and effectuate its own licenses if the contractor has "not taken, or is not expected to take within a reasonable time, effective steps to achieve practical application of the subject invention in such field of use.".

13 For an example of a typical license agreement, *See* "Model License Agreement: Exclusive License Agreement Between The Johns Hopkins University & ____," *reprinted in* Technology Transfer Issues for Colleges and Universities: A Legal Compendium (Judith L. Curry, ed., National Association of College and University Attorneys (NACUA) 2005) at 265.

tions. Specifically, the universities must *license* their federally funded inventions, since they are prohibited from *assigning* any rights to any for-profit entity.[14] The prohibition on assignments relates to the general idea that the university should do as much as possible to ensure that an invention is serving the public, and by transferring ownership, the university would lose control over the practicing of the invention.[15]

B. History of the Bayh-Dole Act

To understand the rationale for the provisions of Bayh-Dole and the consequences of the Act, a brief history of the university technology transfer system and other relevant circumstances leading to the passing of this Act is instructive.

1. Historical Characteristics of the United States Higher Education System

R&D originating from universities in the U.S. carries many characteristics unique from the systems of other countries. The pathway to such distinct innovation has its roots in the early twentieth century. The U.S. university system enrolled a larger fraction of eighteen to twenty-two year olds than any European nation from 1900 onwards.[16] The most developed European countries did not reach this level until the 1960s, at which point the U.S. already had nearly half of this age group attending a higher-level institution.[17]

Included in many universities' curricula was a vast amount of specialized engineering coursework, often specifically tailored to the needs of a certain region.[18] The ability for students and researchers to work on projects that could contribute to a local interest and solve practical problems was an automatic incentive to innovate and a costless motivational tool.[19]

The U.S. higher education system can be further distinguished from other countries with respect to its unified and competitive national market for faculty.[20] Euro-

14 *See* 35 U.S.C. § 202(c)(7)(a) (2009). This policy behind this provision underlines an expectation of the government for the university to retain certain control over the invention, which is complicated by the *Stanford v. Roche* decision and discussed in Chapter V-B-4-b, *infra*. For definitions of licenses and assignments, *see* note 8, *supra*.

15 However, an exclusive license is permitted, so long as the title remains with the university. *See* Kettner and Decker, *supra* note 6 at 15.

16 *See* Mowery, *supra* note 5, at 18.

17 *See id.* at 11.

18 *See id.* at 12.

19 *See id.* at 14.

20 *See id.* at 13.

pean universities tended to appoint their own graduates to faculty positions, and rarely recruited from outside. Conversely, American universities recruited faculty from numerous sources and maintained a competitive marketplace.[21] This increased mobility motivated researchers to seek commercial applications for inventions and allowed for the diffusion of new ideas and novel research approaches.[22]

2. The Growth of Federal Funding on Academic Research

The priorities of the federal government with respect to general R&D shifted once the U.S. entered into World War II, and these expenditures increased fifteen-fold between 1940 and 1945.[23]

The renewed interest in R&D during the war incentivized the government to augment its focus on university grants, since university researchers included some of the brightest and most innovative minds in the country. Between 1935 and 1960, the overall academic research enterprise increased nearly six-fold.[24] The federal grant money was used to support broad explorations of uncertain technologies and growth areas, which ultimately led to major breakthroughs in previously under-researched areas, including biomedical and aeronautical engineering.[25]

3. University Patenting and Patent Policy Trends Prior to Bayh-Dole

While some universities began to patent faculty inventions as early as the 1920s, formal patent policies were mostly a product of the post World War II era.[26] Considerable and steady growth of patenting by universities was seen in the 1970s and in the years leading to the passing of Bayh-Dole.

A sea change in invention management occurred in the two decades leading to Bayh-Dole.[27] Pursuant to this transformation, many U.S. universities began not only to seek patents for faculty inventions, but also to manage their patent and licensing activities.[28] Since the government retained title to federally-funded in-

21 *See* Hugh Davis Graham and Nancy Diamond, THE RISE OF AMERICAN RESEARCH UNIVERSITIES, (Baltimore: Johns Hopkins University Press, 1997) at 20.

22 *See* Mowery, *supra* note 5 at 13.

23 *See id.* at 22.

24 *Id.* at 23.

25 *Id.* at 26.

26 *Id.* at 35.

27 *Id.* at 44. This change was led by the creation of the Research Corporation, which administered inventions for over 200 institutions in 1970. The corporation encouraged and assisted universities in managing early stage technology transfer. *See id.*

28 *Id., citing* C. Weiner, *Universities, Professors and Patents: A Continuing Controversy,* TECH. REV. 83 at 33-43.

ventions prior to the passing of the BDA, newly motivated universities began to petition the government for title. In the 1970s, the government would hear these petitions only on a case-by-case basis.[29]

Though universities engaged in technology transfer on a limited scale in the 1970s, the process was complex and confusing.[30] Each government agency had its own policies and procedural requirements with respect to technology transfer, and the vast majority of patents went unlicensed.[31]

4. Birth of Bayh-Dole

Prior to the BDA, the government owned the title to any federally funded invention. Ownership included the exclusive right to develop, market, and license the invention.[32] The agencies that maintained title over these inventions often were unable to fully commercialize the invention, which led to underutilized patents and suboptimal public benefit.[33] Furthermore, the government often made it difficult for companies to gain an exclusive license to the invention, which hampered the ability to fully explore and market the idea.[34]

The 95th Congress had been wrestling with the recommendation that legislation to develop a reliable and uniform technology transfer mechanism should be created.[35] Congress and President Jimmy Carter advocated a change to ensure that those receiving federal funds had a greater ability to commercialize inventions and contribute more to society.[36] Senators Bayh and Dole created a bill to be a compromise

29 *See* David C. Mowery and Bhaven Sampat, *University Patents and Policy Debates: 1925-1980*, prepared for Conference at Columbia University, October 13-15, 2000, *available at* professor-murmann.net/nelsonfest/moweryp.doc.

30 *See* The Bayh-Dole Act at 25: BayhDole25, Inc., April 17, 2006, at 2.

31 *See id.* at 2.

32 *See* Office of Technology and Transfer and Economic Development. What is the Bayh-Dole Act, What Prompted it, and Why is it important to University Technology Transfer? University of Hawaii., *available at* http://www.otted.hawaii.edu/what-bayh-dole-act.

33 *See* Marcia Boumil and Harris Berman. Revisiting the Physician/Industry Alliance: The Bayh-Dole Act and Conflict of Interest Management at Academic Medical Centers. 15 MICH. STATE UNIV. OF MEDICINE & LAW 1 (2010). The government agencies often lacked the resources, expertise and relationships with industry necessary to commercialize the inventions created under governmental funding.

34 *See* Innovation's golden goose, *supra* note 4. Additionally, the difficulty in acquiring exclusive rights made it uneconomical for a company to invest their own money in bringing an idea from general invention to commercial success.

35 *See* Boumil and Berman, *supra* note 33, at 2.

36 *See* Ralph C. Nash and Leonard Rawicz, INTELLECTUAL PROPERTY IN GOVERNMENT CONTRACTS 238 (The George Washington University 6 ed.) (2008). President Carter originally wanted title to stay with the government, but exclusive licenses to be granted to the Contractor. He changed his stance upon noting that if small businesses and nonprofits (including universities) retained title to their inventions, this would not stymie commercialization. *See id.*

of sorts: under the original bill, the possibility for a shift of title away from the government would occur only in the case of universities and small businesses.[37]

Shortly prior to the passing of the BDA, Congress noted that "many new discoveries and advances in science occur in universities and federal laboratories, while the application of this new knowledge to commercial and useful public purposes depends largely upon actions by business and labor."[38] Furthermore, Congress stated that cooperation among academia, industry, and the government is vital and should be expanded and strengthened.[39]

Pursuant to its own findings, Congress passed the Patent and Trademark Law Amendments Act ("Bayh-Dole Act") with minimal conflict on December 12, 1980, and President Carter signed the legislation into law shortly thereafter.[40]

37 *See* Mowery et al., *supra* note 5, at 89. This compromise satisfied the executive branch of the Government as well as the members of Congress who fought against similar proposals that transferred ownership away from the government in all federally funded inventions. However, President Reagan in 1983 signed an amendment stating that the Act "is not intended to limit the authority of agencies to agree with to the disposition of rights in inventions... with persons other than nonprofit organizations or small business firms." 35 U.S.C. § 210(c). This significantly widened the scope of the Act and effectively ensured that disposition of *all* federally funded inventions can be dealt with under this scheme. *See* Kevin W. McCabe, IMPLICATIONS OF THE CELLPRO DETERMINATION ON INVENTIONS MADE WITH FEDERAL ASSISTANCE: WILL THE GOVERNMENT EVER EXERCISE ITS MARCH-IN RIGHT? 27 PUB. CONT. L.J. 645, 652 (1998).

38 *See* 15 U.S.C.A. § 3701 (2011).

39 *See* 15 U.S.C.A. § 3701(2011). Congress further notes that no comprehensive national policy to enhance technological innovation currently existed, and that such a policy would "reduce trade deficits, stabilize the dollar, increase productivity gains, increase employment, and stabilize prices." *Id.*

40 *See* Nash and Rawicz, *supra* note 36, at 237; Mowery et al., *supra* note 5, at 91.

II. Statutory Provisions of the Bayh-Dole Act

A. *Introductory Provisions*

1. Policy and Scope of the Act

The BDA's enumerated policy objectives are codified in 35 U.S.C. § 200.[41] Despite the objective of encouraging private industry to utilize government funded inventions and bring them to commercial applicability, the BDA does not specifically affect the patentability of an invention.[42] Patents are subject to the patentability requirements of 35 U.S.C. §§ 101, 102, 103 and 112.[43] The Federal Circuit rejected an argument that government funded inventions should be subject to lesser requirements, stating that "The Bayh-Dole Act was intended to enable universities to profit from their federally-funded research. It was not intended to relax the statutory requirements for patentability."[44]

It is further notable that the scope of the BDA has been recently interpreted not to affect the general patent policy that title to the invention vests in the actual inventor. The Supreme Court recently adjudged a case that proposed that the BDA effectively reordered the "hierarchy," and that title automatically vests in the universities for federally funded inventions. The court rejected this argument and determined that ownership vests in the inventor, regardless of whether or not an invention is federally funded.[45]

41 The statute states: " It is the policy and objective of the Congress to use the patent system to promote the utilization of inventions arising from federally supported research or development; to encourage maximum participation of small business firms in federally supported research and development efforts; to promote collaboration between commercial concerns and nonprofit organizations, including universities; to ensure that inventions made by nonprofit organizations and small business firms are used in a manner to promote free competition and enterprise without unduly encumbering future research and discovery; to promote the commercialization and public availability of inventions made in the United States by United States industry and labor; to ensure that the government obtains sufficient rights in federally supported inventions to meet the needs of the government and protect the public against nonuse or unreasonable use of inventions; and to minimize the costs of administering policies in this area." 35 U.S.C. § 200 (2009).

42 *See* Nash and Rawicz, *supra* note 36, at 246.

43 These statutes are the general rules relating to patentability, notably § 101 governing patentable subject matter and utility, § 102 governing novelty, § 103 governing nonobviousness, and § 112 governing enablement, written description, and best mode. See 35 U.S.C. §§ 101-103, 112 (2008).

44 Univ. of Rochester v. G.D. Searle & Co., 358 F.3d 916, 929 (Fed. Cir, 2004).

45 *See* Stanford, *supra* note 10. A detailed discussion of this landmark case and its implications in the field of university technology transfer is discussed in Chapter V, *infra*.

2. Definitions

The Act seeks to further identify its scope by defining terms that ultimately govern when the Act should apply. Of note, the BDA applies only for funding by federal agencies for "the performance of experimental, developmental, or research work funded in whole or in part[46] by the federal government."[47]

A subject invention[48] is any invention of the contractor "conceived or first actually reduced to practice in the performance of work under a funding agreement...."[49] The use and placement of the term "contractor" ensures that the reduction to practice relates to the contractor's invention, and that work of a contractor reducing someone else's invention to practice would not qualify as a "subject invention."[50]

B. Disposition of Rights

The disposition of rights contemplated under Bayh-Dole is codified in 35 U.S.C. § 202. This specifically allows for the contractor to retain title from the government.[51] For the contractor to achieve this, it must undertake several procedural steps, including a disclosure and an election.[52]

1. The Disclosure and Election

§ 202(a) of the Act requires the contractor to make an affirmative election that it wishes to gain the title to a subject invention. Furthermore, the BDA imposes four exceptions that give the government the option to override the contractor's option

46 Thus, the project need not be entirely funded by government money. *See* Nash and Rawicz, *supra* note 36, at 255.
47 35 U.S.C. § 201(a-b) (2009). A federal agency is any executive agency as defined in 5 U.S.C. § 105 or the military departments under 5 U.S.C. § 102. A funding agreement is "any contract, grant or cooperative agreement entered into between any Federal agency....".
48 *See* 35 U.S.C. § 201(e) (2009) (subject invention); *See* 35 U.S.C. § 201(d)(2009) (invention).
49 35 U.S.C. § 201(e) (2009).
50 *See* Nash and Rawicz, *supra* note 36, at 258.
51 *See* 35 U.S.C. § 202 (2009).
52 *See* Nash and Rawicz, *supra* note 36, at 266.

to retain title.[53] Thus, title is not automatically vested in the contractor pursuant to the Act.

First, the contractor must disclose each subject invention to the federal agency providing the funding within a reasonable time once it becomes aware of the invention.[54] Failure to disclose promptly provides the government with adequate means to forfeit the award of title to a contractor.[55]

The contractor also must make a written election to the federal agency within two years of disclosure.[56] This election should maintain that the contractor will agree to file a patent application prior to any statutory bar date and further file corresponding patent applications in other countries where it wishes to retain title.[57]

2. Contractor Failure to Elect Title

§ 202(d) of the Act states that "[i]f a contractor does not elect to retain title... the Federal agency may consider and after consultation with the contractor grant requests for retention of the rights by the inventor subject to the provisions of this Act."[58] The language of this provision implies two important concepts: that a subject invention is still subject to the other requirements of Bayh-Dole even if the contractor does not elect to take title, and that the inventor may not automatically retain rights over the government to an invention he created.[59] The Supreme Court

53 *See id.* at 267. It is notable that the exceptions do not automatically preclude a contractor from making an election or even having it granted; they are merely optional bases for the federal agency to refuse to give title to the contractor. *See* 35 U.S.C. § 202(a). However, if no exceptions exist, the government cannot otherwise preclude a contractor from making an election of title *See* 35 U.S.C. § 202(b) (2009).

54 *See* 35 U.S.C. § 202(c)(1)(2009); *See* Nash and Rawicz, *supra* note 36, at 267.

55 *See* Campbell Plastics Eng. v. Brownlee, 389 F.3d 1243, 1250 (Fed. Cir. 2004).

56 *See 35 U.S.C.* § 202(c)(2) (2009). The statute notes that the period for election may be shortened if publication, sale or public use has initiated a statutory bar period under 35 U.S.C. § 102.

57 *See* 35 U.S.C. § 202(c)(3) (2009). The government may receive title to subject inventions in the U.S. or any other country in which the contract has not filed a patent application on the subject invention within a reasonable time.

58 35 U.S.C. § 202(d) (2009).

59 However, the language of the statute does not prevent patent rights clauses from providing the contractor with revocable licenses in subject inventions. *See* Nash and Rawicz, *supra* note 36 , at 317. Therefore, the government not only may not be able to exercise full title because of the rights of the inventor, but it must also license certain rights to the contractor.

recently dealt with the latter issue, and this will be discussed in Chapters V, *infra.*[60]

C. *Government Rights*

1. Non-Exclusive License

The funding federal agency gains, at a minimum, a nonexclusive license to practice for or on behalf of the United States and subject invention throughout the world.[61] This provision has been criticized by some as being too narrow in international scope, and by others as too broad with respect to available uses.[62] Additionally, the license refers to the subject invention itself and not to the rights in patents covering such inventions.[63] Thus, a government license on a patentable product that was derived from a federally funded invention may not cover the use of all claims, and in effect may make full use of the patentable product impossible.

2. March-in Rights

One of the most contentious provisions of Bayh-Dole is the allowance for a government agency to "march in" and perform actions on an invention if the action is necessary because of any one of four enumerated situations. The funding agency can, under explicit circumstances, require the contractor to grant licenses or even to grant the licenses itself.[64] The effect of the march-in provision is to ensure that the government still has the ability to ensure an invention is achieving the policy

60 The Supreme Court noted in *Stanford v. Roche* that this (or any other) provision of Bayh-Dole does not reorder the "well-established" hierarchy of patent rights: absent an assignment of his rights, the title to the invention is initially vested in the inventor himself. *See* Stanford, *supra* note 10.

61 *See* 35 U.S.C. § 202(c)(4) (2009). The license is further irrevocable, nonexclusive, and paid up. *See* Nash and Rawicz, *supra* note 36, at 310.

62 *See* Nash and Rawicz, *supra* note 36, at 311. "Some argue that this license is too broad in that it applies to all federal agencies for all uses and not just for the funding agency's use; others view this license as too narrow, as this license should be available to international health organizations... so that developing countries may be able to obtain the drugs at acceptable costs.".

63 *See id.* at 313.

64 The most relevant of these circumstances are the lack of the contractor taking steps to achieve practical application of the subject invention and to alleviate health or safety needs. *See* 35 U.S.C. § 203 (2009); *See* Nash and Rawicz, *supra* note 36, at 330.

purpose of, among others, "promoting the commercialization and public available of inventions made in the United States by United States industry and labor."[65]

To encourage the government to use its march-in right, an adversely affected party can file a petition, detailing the specific reasons that would justify the government agency to march-in (and typically grant a license to the affected party).[66] While a number of petitions have been filed in the past quarter-century, the government has consistently refused to grant the petitions and.[67] Despite the government's lack of utilization of its march-in rights, it contends that the provision is effective since it provides leverage to promote commercialization of federally funded inventions.[68] Many other scholars and some government agencies disagree with respect to the effectiveness of the provision.[69] A detailed analysis of the effect of this provision will be discussed in Chapter IV, *infra.*

D. Implied Duty to Commercialize

While it is not explicitly stated in the statute, an analysis of the above provisions denotes an implied duty to commercialize levied on the contractor. First, the goal is explicitly mentioned in Bayh-Dole's policy objectives.[70] Secondly, the option to retain title to a subject invention triggers various requirements and responsibili-

65 35 U.S.C. § 200 (2009).

66 For an example petition, *See* Joseph M. Carik et al., "PETITION TO USE AUTHORITY UNDER THE BAYH-DOLE ACT TO PROMOTE ACCESS TO FABRYZYME (AGALSIDASE BETA), AN INVENTION SUPPORTED BY AND LICENSED BY THE NATIONAL INSTITUTES OF HEALTH UNDER GRANT NO. DK-34045, *available at* http://www.genomicslawreport.com/wp-content/uploads/2011/01/Fabrazyme-Bayh-Dole-Petition.pdf. This petition was subsequently denied. *See* John Conley, Government Refused to March-In Under Bayh-Dole – Again, Genomics Law Report, January 8, 2011, *available at* http://www.genomicslawreport.com/index.php/2011/01/18/government-refuses-to-march-in-under-bayh-dole-again/.

67 As of January 2011, the National Institute of Health has never granted a march-in petition under the public health provision or any other provision of § 203. *See* Conley, *supra* note 66.

68 *See* GAO Rep. No. 09-742, at 10-11, *reprinted at* http://www.gao.gov/htext/d09742.html, *hereinafter* GAO Report. The Government Accountability Office performed a study with respect to the effectiveness of the march-in provision and published its findings in 2009.

69 *See id.* at 11; *See generally* News Release, Duke University, Patent policy flaws complicate commercialization of federally funded university discoveries (December 11, 2002) *available at* http://www.eurekaalert.org/pub_releases/2002-12/du-ppfl120602.php.

70 *See* 35 U.S.C. § 200 (2009). A policy goal is to promote the commercialization and public availability of inventions.

ties.[71] Finally, the march-in provision implies that the contractor is under a duty to commercialize, as failure to do so can result in government intervention.[72]

71 *See* Jennifer A. Henderson and John J. Smith, Academia, Industry and the Bayh-Dole Act: An Implied Duty to Commercialize, paper supported in part by a grant from the Center for Integration of Medicine and Innovative Technology (CIMIT), at 4. Specifically, under 202(c), contractors must agree to file a patent application before any statutory bar date, and failure to do so may result in title forfeiture. Also under 202(c), contractors must report to the federal funding agency on the efforts at obtaining utilization.

72 *See* 35 U.S.C. § 203 (2009). The government can march-in if, for example, "the contractor or assignee has not taken... effective steps to achieve practical application of the subject invention.".

III. Perceived Successes and Shortfalls of the Bayh-Dole Act

This chapter will deal with the perceived strengths and weaknesses of the BDA, as contemplated by academics and practitioners. Chapter IV will analyze these perceptions and assess the effect of the statute on university technology transfer.

A. Perceived Successes of the Bayh-Dole Act

1. Single, Uniform Policy

Even those most critical of Bayh-Dole admit that the Act offers a single and uniform policy which government agencies and contractors must abide by.[73] In its legislative report commemorating the twenty-fifth anniversary of Bayh-Dole, Congress noted that Bayh-Dole successfully established a "single, uniform national policy designed to... encourage private industry to utilize government financed inventions through the commitment of the risk capital necessary to develop such inventions to the point of commercial application."[74] This has allowed for more uniformity across agencies and less confusion between all associated entities, which can only benefit the technology transfer process.

73 However, these critics note that at least some provisions of Bayh-Dole allow for different agencies and contractors to behave in different manners. For example, Arti Rai and Rebecca Eisenberg explain that the "exceptional circumstances" from which agencies can depart from the typical "title to contractor" presumption are vague. By stating the agency can only exercise its power "infrequently," the standard is constraining the policy goal of "promoting widespread dissemination and use of research results" and thus allows for inconsistent actions across Government agencies. *See generally* Arti K. Rai and Rebecca S. Eisenberg, *The Public Domain: Bayh-Dole Reform and the Progress and Biomedicine*, 66 Law and Contemp. Probs. 289 (2003). Critics also contend that the march-in rights provision can be construed differently across different agencies, despite the fact that no agency has fully used its march-in rights to date. *See* Duke News Release, *supra* note 69 (noting that the NIH has extreme flexibility to make a determination as to whether or not to march-in pursuant to the Bayh-Dole Act).

74 H.R. Con. Res. 319, 109th Cong. (2005), at 2, *reprinted in* H.R. Rep. No. 109-409 at 7. Congress issued this report and resolution ultimately to reaffirm that Bayh-Dole has "made substantial contributions to the advancement of scientific knowledge,... " and to ensure that Congress continues to uphold its commitment to the policies and objectives of the Act. *See id.* at 11-12.

2. Increase in Patents. Cooperative Ventures, and Commercial Products

One of the major issues inherent in successful technology transfer is that private industry requires that government funded inventions be patented to justify the expenditure of resources to develop an invention into commercial applicability.[75] Proponents of Bayh-Dole maintain that there has been a substantial increase in both the number of patents and cooperative ventures between universities and other companies pursuant to the Act. In 1980, fewer than 250 patents were issued to US universities annually; in 2003, there were 3933.[76]

Congress noted in their 2006 report that the Act has "resulted in new cooperative ventures and the emergence of sophisticated high-technology businesses, which provide a major catalyst for innovation and entrepreneurial activity."[77] Since 1980, it has been estimated that the licensing of inventions has added $40 billion to the domestic economy and has been responsible for creating 260,000 new jobs.[78] These numbers are in stark contrast to the pre-Bayh-Dole scheme, where only a small percentage of the estimated 28,000-30,000 Government owned patents had been successfully licensed and exploited.[79]

3. The Emergence of the Biotechnology Field

Another perceived success of the Bayh-Dole Act is apparent from the emergence of the biotechnology field over the past quarter-century. Research indicates that the major share of university patents is related to biomedical research.[80] The Association of University Technology Managers (hereinafter AUTM) has found that 70%

75 *See* Michael S. Mireles, *Adoption of the Bayh-Dole Act in Developed Countries: Added Pressure for a Broad Research Exemption in the United States?*, 59 ME. L. REV. 259, 263 (2007). The requirement of a contractor electing rights to file a patent application helps achieve this goal. 35 U.S.C. § 202(c)(3) (2009).

76 *See* Bayh Dole at 25, *supra* note 30 , at page 23. Also, a much higher percentage of patents are being successfully commercialized, and licensing has increased dramatically. Critics take issue with such direct comparison of the pre and post-Bayh-Dole numbers; their views regarding the numbers will be discussed later in this chapter, and an analysis of the true effect Bayh-Dole has had on the increase will be discussed in Chapter IV, *infra.*

77 *See* House Resolution, *supra* note 74 , at 9. At least 4081 university start-up companies have been created since the Bayh-Dole Act's conception. *See* Bayh-Dole Act at 25, *supra* note 30 , at 23; *See* Chester G. Moore, *Killing the Bayh-Dole Act's Golden Goose,* 8 TUL. L. J. TECH. & INTELL. PROP. 151, 155 (2006);.

78 *See* Moore, supra note 77, at 156.

79 *See* Rebecca S. Eisenberg, *Symposium on Regulating Medical Innovation: Public Research and Private Development: Patents and Technology Transfer in Government-Sponsored Research*, 82 VA. L. REV. 1663, 1702 (1996). Eisenberg notes, however, that these numbers may be attributed to a "selection bias" of sorts and that many of these inventions were commercially irrelevant, period. *See id.* at 1703.

80 *See* Rai and Eisenberg, *supra* note 73, at 292.

of the inventions it recognizes are related to biotechnology.[81] Since the majority of these inventions are also publicly funded, Bayh-Dole has proved to be highly important in this field.[82]

Though one may be able to concede that Bayh-Dole did not explicitly create the biotechnology revolution, the incentives it provides are critical for promoting innovation in this field.[83] The biotechnology field necessarily carries high research and development costs,[84] which is well addressed by Bayh-Dole's policy objective of encouraging maximum participation of small business firms in research and development efforts, and in promoting collaboration between commercial entities and nonprofit organizations.[85] There are now close to 200,000 Americans employed in the biotech field, which is a number that can be at least partially attributed to the Bayh-Dole Act.[86]

B. *Perceived Shortfalls of the Bayh-Dole Act*

1. It Would Have Happened Anyway

One of the more popular critiques of the Bayh-Dole Act is the wealth of attention it receives is undeserved. Commentators note that university patents had been on the rise in the years prior to Bayh-Dole.[87] Thus, Bayh-Dole has been evaluated as an effect more than a cause of university patent successes.[88] Critics also contend

81 *See* Bayh-Dole at 25, *supra* note 30, at 24. The article further explains that biotechnology was a field that was "in its infancy" prior to Bayh-Dole.

82 *See* Rai and Eisenberg, *supra* note 73 at 292. Rai and Eisenberg later argue that Bayh-Dole limits the government's ability to oversee the use of intellectual property rights, in ultimately suggesting a modification of Bayh-Dole. *See* id at 293-294. An analysis of proposed changes to Bayh-Dole with respect to march-in will follow in Chapter IV, *infra.*

83 *See* Bayh-Dole at 25, *supra* note 30, at 24.

84 *See* Esteban Burrone, *Patents at the Core: the Biotech Business*, World Intellectual Property Office, *available at* http://www.wipo.int/sme/en/documents/patents_biotech.htm. Burrone notes that the facts that the biotech field are so research intensive and carry such high R&D costs for new products, coupled with the low cost of imitation by competitors, leads the industry to be highly patent dependent. *Id.*

85 *See* 35 U.S.C. § 200 (2009). Congress has further explicitly noted that Bayh-Dole has "stimulated... the development of the biotechnology and information communication industries" and notes that it is poised to play a role in nanotechnology, another area with very high research and development costs. *See* House Resolution, *supra* note 74, at 8.

86 *See* Mireles, *supra* note 75, at 264.

87 *See id.* at 265. A variable that may have led to a rise in university patenting includes the creation of the Federal Circuit as a court with exclusive jurisdiction on patent claims. *Id.* at 265.

88 *See* Mowery, *supra* note 5, at 97.

that the "celebratory analysis" in the popular press lacks hard evidence, as studies do not explain how the effects have been attributed to Bayh-Dole.[89]

Critics also take specific issue with the contention that Bayh-Dole spurred the biotechnology industry. Mowery et al. show that biomedical technology had increased significantly by the 1970s, and the *Chakrabarty* decision and shifts in intellectual property rights policy increased the economic value of these patents.[90] Thus, Bayh-Dole should be seen as only one of many variables leading to the biotechnology boom in the latter part of the twentieth century.

2. Undermining Research, Development, and Technology Transfer

Rai and Eisenberg argue that Bayh-Dole actually undermines the flow of biomedical research for several reasons.[91] First, "patents on upstream discoveries... [permit] owners to charge a premium for the use of discoveries that might otherwise be more cheaply available in a competitive market or in the public domain."[92] Essentially, Bayh-Dole's requirement on the contractor to patent the early stage invention will unreasonably raise the price for another entity to use the discovery and ultimately benefit the public.[93] Rai and Eisenberg also explain that upstream patenting could hinder subsequent research because a single entity will have monopoly control of basic research discoveries across a broad field.[94] Furthermore, the high costs of patent management may hinder technology transfer as the costs

89 *See id.* However, empirical studies and analysis have been performed on this topic, and will be analyzed in Chapter IV, *infra.*

90 *See id.* at 127-128. The *Chakrabaty* case was a Supreme Court decision widening the scope of patentable subject matter, especially with respect to genetically modified organisms. *See* Diamond v. Chakrabarty, 447 U.S. 303 (1979).

91 *See* Rai and Eisenberg, *supra* note 73. The major contentions in this article can be superimposed to relate to all fields of patenting, though those with higher R&D costs are more likely to be affected by the commentators' arguments.

92 *Id.* at 295.

93 However, critics to this argument state that without patents to permit pricing above the marginal cost, no one would be motivated to incur the R&D expenses to innovate to begin with. *See id.* at 296. It has also been posited that Bayh-Dole amounts to the public being required to "double-pay." Because the inventions are publicly funded, the public incurs a cost at the research phase. Then, because of the patent, the contractor is able charge a monopoly price, effectively charging the public again. *See* Gary Pulsinelli, *Share and Share Alike: Increasing Access to Government-Funded Inventions Under the Bayh-Dole Act*, 7 MINN J.L. SCI. & TECH 393, 410-411 (2006).

94 *See* Rai and Eisenberg, *supra* note 73 , at 296. This is particularly important for patents on early-stage discoveries that open up new research fields as they would be quite broad and lead to monopolistic control over a large range of issues.

limit "the financial returns from patent licensing."[95] Additionally, licensing becomes difficult because of valuation problems in early stage inventions that universities are forced to try and commercialize under Bayh-Dole.[96]

3. Misallocated Research Priorities

A major criticism of Bayh-Dole is that it "distorts research priorities" by "redirecting resources away from basic research to more commercially viable lines of inquiry."[97] Scholars note that the nature and direction of academic research may be compromised due to universities and researchers' conflicting economic incentives.[98] The ultimate concern is that Bayh-Dole will lead to research and development with for-profit motives, and this conflicts with the policies outlined in the Act.[99]

A recent federal court decision may have indirectly criticized Bayh-Dole on these grounds. In *Myriad*, a court rules against multiple biotechnological patents, stating that they were "purifications of a product of nature" and thus do not possess the requisite utility.[100] Though this decision has recently been reversed by the Federal Circuit, commentators note that Myriad "represents an almost caricature-like example of the pitfalls of... technology transfer," as the purpose of the patent was to gain a valuable market commodity, and not to contribute to broader medical research.[101]

95 *See* Mowery et al., *supra* note 5, at 84. The general assertion is that Bayh-Dole's over-incentivizing universities to patent inventions will cause problems in the long run, as the costs incurred in managing the patents will indirectly lead to a higher price in any licensing contract. This would lead to sunk costs and become a disincentive for industries to want to become engaged in technology transfer.

96 *See* Clovia Hamilton, *University Technology Transfer and Economic Development: Proposed Cooperative Economic Development Agreements Under the Bayh-Dole Act,* 36 J. MARSHALL L. REV. 397, 406 (2003). The requirement to patent and the duty to commercialize also lead to "a number of low-value exchanges and agreements that have a low potential of truly yielding anything of commercial value." *Id.*

97 *See* Bayh-Dole at 25, *supra* note 30, at 31. This article continues by rationalizing that the "federal government's funding priorities have also always favored practical applications," in an attempt to demerit the critique of the act.

98 *See* Hamilton, *supra* note 96 at 406.

99 *See* Kathryn R. James, The *Myriad* decision: Judicial criticism of the Bayh-Dole Act and its progeny?, ABA Health eSource Vol 6-10 (June 2010), at page 3.

100 *See* Association for Molecular Pathology et al. v. United States Patent and Trademark Office et al., 702 F. Supp. 2d 181 (S.D.N.Y. 2010), *rev'd in part,* 2011 U.S. App. Lexis 15649 (Fed. Cir, 2011).

101 James, supra note 99, at 3. Commentators note that the Myriad patents were filed to obtain exclusive control over uses of a particular gene for profit. This maneuver arguably did not contribute to the "public good" and was provoked solely by economic motives. *See id.*

These misallocated priorities can ultimately lead to a complete market failure. A similar criticism invites the analysis that the incentives of Bayh-Dole move research away from socially critical industries, such as cures for rare diseases.[102] Hence, the BDA arguably may not be achieving what some believe to be an important objective of contributing to the public welfare.

4. The "Anticommons" Effect

The metaphor "tragedy of the commons" was developed in 1968 when Garrett Hardin attempted to explain some biological and ecological phenomena.[103] The theory states that when people own a resource in common, they will overuse because there is no incentive to conserve.[104]

The "tragedy of the anticommons" is the converse of that theory, and it applies particularly in patenting. The theory states if there are multiple owners, each has a right to exclude others from a scarce resource. Thus, no one has an effective privilege of use.[105] Thus, patented technologies are ultimately underused and not commercialized. While this problem occurs in patenting generally, it is particularly prevalent in the biotechnology field, where patents are incredibly important, transaction costs of trading patents are very high, and future discoveries build upon past discoveries.[106] Commentators argue that Bayh-Dole exacerbates the anticommons problem with its practical consequence of increased early stage patenting of discoveries that would have been left to the public domain absent Bayh-Dole.[107] This hypothesis will be further studied in chapter *IV-B, infra.*

102 *See* Bayh Dole at 25, *supra* note 30 , at 28. The article continues by stating that even though Bayh-Dole may not have specifically incentivized "less profitable" research areas, other Acts of Congress, such as orphan drug legislation, have responded to the issue. *Id.*

103 *See* Michael A. Heller and Rebecca S. Eisenberg, *Can Patents Deter Innovation? The Anticommons in Biomedical Research,* Science, Vol. 280, 1 May 1998, at 698. This metaphor is now a central theory in economics, law and science.

104 *See* Pulsinelli, *supra* note 93, at 415.

105 *Id.* Thus, these scare resources (specifically patented inventions) are prone to *under*use. *See* Rachel A. Ream, Nonprofit Commercialization Under Bayh-Dole and the Academic Anticommons, 58 Case W. Res. L. Rev. 1343, 1347 (2008).

106 *See* Ream, *supra* note 105, at 1347-1348.

107 *See* Pulsinelli, *supra* note 93, at 416. Another similar effect may be presented if both researchers and universities can assert rights because Bayh-Dole does not limit this possibility. This will be further explored in the analysis of *Stanford* in Chapter V, *infra.*

IV. Effectiveness of the Bayh-Dole Act

This chapter will analyze two particular areas of the Bayh-Dole statute and use case studies and empirical evidence to determine their effects on the university technology transfer system. The areas of focus include the march-in provision and the general shift of title towards the universities.

A. Is the March-In Right Provision (§ 203) Effective?

The march-in provision invites criticism from both sides of the spectrum; while some consider the march-in right contrary to the very premise of the transfer of ownership away from the government,[108] many criticize the provision as too infrequently used and unable to assist the government in ensuring an invention gets commercialized.[109]

Congress codified the march-in provision because it considered the government's "free and irrevocable license" insufficient to protect the "public's need for competition in the marketplace."[110] Industry disapproved of the provision, citing that "it is not a good concept that government should go into competition with private enterprise."[111] Though there have been several march-in petitions to various

108 For views criticizing march-in rights as contravening the premise of Bayh-Dole, see Peter Arno & Michael Davis, *Why Don't We Enforce Existing Drug Price Controls? The Unrecognized and Unenforced Reasonable Pricing Requirements Imposed upon Patents Deriving in Whole or in Part from Federally Funded Research*, 75 TULANE L. REV. 631, 661 (2001), *citing* Patent Policy: Joint Hearing Before the S. Comm. on Commerce, Sci., & Transp. & the S. Comm. on the Judiciary, 96th Cong. 458-60 (1980), (testimony of Robert B. Benson, Dir., Patent Dep't, Allis-Chalmers Corp.); *see* Barbara M. McGarey & Annette C. Levey, *Patents, Products, and Public Health: An Analysis of the CellPro March-in Petition,* 14 BERKLEY TECH L.J. 1095, 1109-1113 (1999) (denouncing the march-in provision as procedurally burdensome and as an unwieldy safeguard).

109 For a view criticizing the government's nonuse of the march-in provision, s*ee* Conley, *supra* note 66 (arguing government's failure to grant march-in rights in CellPro case was dubious); *see* Rai and Eisenberg, *supra* note 73 (stating that the requirement that march-in requires exhaustion of all court appeals by the contractor should be changed).

110 Arno and Davis, *supra* note , at 660.

111 *Id.* at 661.

agencies over the years, the chief agencies dealing with university-owned patents have never exercised any rights under the provision.[112]

1. Cases in Point: CellPro, Fabrazyme, and the Government Refusal to March-in

Over the past two decades, four petitions to the National Institute of Health (hereinafter NIH) involving a march-in request have been heard: *CellPro, Norvir, Pfizer, and Fabyrzyme.* The NIH has denied each petition.[113] A brief review of *CellPro*, the most known and heavily criticized refusal, and *Fabyrzyme,* the most recent decision, bring to light some major concerns regarding the (non)use of the march-in right.

a) The 1997 CellPro Decision

Johns Hopkins University (hereinafter JHU) developed a biotechnological invention with federal funding from the NIH.[114] Ultimately, the patent on the invention ("Civin") was licensed by JHU to Baxter, a biotechnology company which performed work related to stem cell selection.[115]

CellPro, a potential competitor in the market, had negotiations with Baxter but was not awarded a license, and was ultimately sued and found liable for patent infringement.[116] CellPro proceeded to petition the NIH to march-in and grant it a license based upon 35 USC § 203 (1) and (2).[117] At the time, CellPro had the only licensed and marketable end-product based off this patent available in the U.S.[118]

NIH rejected CellPro's decision on both grounds. With respect to the first ground, the NIH noted that Baxter had taken the requisite steps to achieve practical

112 *See* David Halperin, *The Bayh-Dole Act and March-in Rights*, May 2001, prepared at the request of Consumer Project on Technology, *available at* http://www.ott.nih.gov/policy/meeting/David-Halperin-Attorney-Counselor.pdf. Recent publications have affirmed the fact that march-in has still not been granted, despite numerous petitions. *See* Posting of J. Steven Rutt to Nano & Cleantech Blog, http://www.nanocleantechblog.com/2010/04/articles/legislation/federal-government-clarifies-marchin-rights-under-bayhdole-system/ (April 23, 2010). For examples of the petition and march-in granting procedure, see Chapter II, *supra.*

113 *See* Conley, *supra* note 66.

114 *See* Determination in the Case of Petition of CellPro, Inc. (Nat'l Inst. Of Health, 1997) at 3, *hereinafter* "NIH-CellPro", *available at* http://www.nih.gov/news/pr/aug97/nihb-01.htm.

115 *See* NIH-CellPro, *supra* note 114, at 3.

116 *See id.*

117 The two grounds were that Baxter had not taken or was not expected to take effective steps to achieve practical application, and that there exists a health or safety need which needs to be alleviated. *See* 35 U.S.C. § 203(a)(1-2) (2009); *See* NIH-CellPro, *supra* note 114, at 3.

118 *See* NIH-CellPro, *supra* note 114, at 4.

application of the subject invention.[119] Specifically, Baxter had developed a prototype, filed for pre-market Approval with the FDA, and was licensing and developing the technology.[120]

The NIH had considerably more trouble rejecting the second ground. In denying the petition, the NIH stated that it is "premature, and inappropriate, for NIH to substitute its judgment for that of clinicians and patients seeking to avail themselves of an FDA-approved medical device."[121] The NIH further noted that Baxter and Hopkins "refrained from enforcing their patent to the full extent of the law," and they weren't effectively stopping CellPro's product from being available.[122] The agency posited that even if CellPro's product becomes less available, there would be no concern as Hopkins and Baxter have "pledged to reasonably satisfy any health need created by the loss of the CellPro product."[123] The NIH hinges on the policy ground that marching in would cause "broader public health implications" which include "the potential loss of new health care products yet to be developed from federally funded research."[124]

Criticism of the CellPro determination is fairly widespread and attacks the march-in provision from all directions. Duke University argued that government should "shoulder more responsibility" for technology that arises from federally funded research.[125] In analyzing the NIH's reluctance to grant the petition, Kevin McCabe forms the argument that the government will never march in.[126] Rai and Eisenberg contend that march-in is not strong enough, and that the NIH should be able to exercise the right more readily.[127] Conversely, McGarey and Levy argue that CellPro highlights the potential danger if march-in *is* ever used, as it may "undermine the process of federal technology transfer by disrupting the existing synergy between the academic community and the private sector.[128]

119 The NIH defines practical application based upon 37 C.F.R. § 404.3(d), specifically "to manufacture... under such conditions as to establish that the invention is being utilized and that its benefits are to the extent permitted by law or Government regulations available to the public on reasonable terms." 35 C.F.R. § 404.3(d) (2006).

120 *See* NIH-CellPro, *supra* note 114, at 4.

121 *Id.*

122 *Id.* at 5. Baxter and Hopkins allowed the injunction to be modified so that "CellPro may continue to make, have made, use and sell... within the United States, until such time as an alternative stem cell concentration device... is approved [by the FDA]." *Id.*

123 *Id.* at 6.

124 *Id.* This argument will be further examined as a weakness of the march-in provision later in this chapter.

125 Duke News Release, *supra* note 69.

126 *See* McCabe, *supra* note 37, at 661.

127 *See* Rai and Eisenberg, *supra* note 73, at 311.

128 McGarey and Levey, *supra* note , at 1116.

b) The 2010 Fabrazyme Decision

The NIH recently denied another petition for march-in.[129] This case involved the only effective and FDA approved treatment for Fabry, a rare disease.[130] In denying a march-in petition, the NIH noted that marching-in would not solve the supply shortage of the drug. It concludes that any competitor would need to seek regulatory approval, which would take longer than it would take for Genzyme (the patentee) to solve the shortage.[131] Furthermore, the NIH notes that no company with a substitute drug has asked Genzyme for a license.[132]

Critics of this decision have determined that NIH has created a "self-fulfilling prophecy" in that no one would even attempt to invest in developing a substitute for the drug until the patent runs out or until a license is guaranteed.[133] Secondly, this refusal to march-in in yet another case sends a signal that the government will never march-in, which would effectively distort the market as contractors will not fear government intervention.[134] Section 3 of this chapter will address many of the concerns addressed by critics of these two decisions.

2. Perceived Advantages of the March-in Provision

The government contends that march-in is more powerful than its nonexclusive license, and will help to ensure commercialization.[135]

As a threshold matter, empirical analysis showing benefits of the march-in provision is nearly impossible to produce, for the simple reason that a march-in petition have never been granted. However, a 2009 GAO report has undertaken to poll numerous officials of agencies, and serves to show some positive opinions regarding the force of the provision.[136]

GAO concluded that while none of the four agencies (DOD DOE NASA and NIH) polled have ever exercised march-in authority, the agencies generally agreed

129 *See* Conley, *supra* note 66.

130 *See id.*

131 *See* Determination in the Case of Fabrazyme (Nat'l Inst. Of Health, 2010) at 1, *hereinafter* "NIH-Fabrazyme", *available at* http://www.ott.nih.gov/policy/March-in-Fabrazyme.pdf.

132 This implied to the NIH that no one had an alternative drug (that would infringe the patent absent a license) available, and thus marching-in would do no good. *See* NIH-Fabrazyme, *supra* note 131 at 9.

133 *See* Conley, *supra* note 66. Thus, by not marching-in, the NIH is limiting the options that will ultimately be available to market.

134 *See id.*

135 *See* McCabe, *supra* note 37, at 653. (noting that a policy of the Act is to ensure the Government obtains sufficient rights to ensure commercialization, in addition to the right to maintain its own license).

136 *See* GAO Report, *supra* note 68, at 10.

that the march-in right amounts to leverage, and should not be abandoned.[137] Specifically, the idea of march-in authority becomes powerful in "informal discussions between contractors and sponsoring agencies and in license negotiations between contractors and potential licensees to encourage commercialization of technologies developed with federal funding."[138] This carries a positive effect on negotiations and implicitly supports Bayh-Dole's policy goal of promoting the commercialization and public availability of inventions.[139] Thus, these agency representatives maintain that the provision has a substantial deterrent effect.

Commentators also argue that there is a valid case for exercising march-in rights, and the provision, as a whole, can be effective.[140] David Halperin states that there are certain technologies, especially in life-saving drugs, where the requirement that the contractor make inventions available "on reasonable terms" should include a reasonable price, and failure to do so would be grounds for an effective march-in.[141]

Though many who advocate for march-in cite the provision's strength as a "scare tactic," Rai and Eisenberg advocate specific benefits of the provision as it relates to biotechnology. The scholars note that allowing march-in as something more than a last resort will effectively reduce delays and ensure that drug and other time-sensitive inventions can get to the public as soon as possible.[142] Advocates of the march-in provision in this regard often point to the "second" condition under § 203, which states that the action is necessary "to alleviate health or safety needs."[143]

Commentators conclude that companies "will not abandon cost-effective technology transfer if an agency exercises march-in rights." These arguments reconcile with Bayh-Dole's goal to ensure that the government can protect the public against nonuse or unreasonable use of inventions.[144]

137 *See id.* at 10-11.
138 *Id.* at 10-11.
139 *See* 35 U.S.C. § 200 (2009).
140 *See generally* Halperin, *supra* note 112; *see generally* Rai and Eisenberg, *supra* note 73.
141 *See* Halperin, *supra* note 112, at 12-13. § 201(f) of the BDA defined "practical application" as found in the march-in provision at § 203(a)(1). Specifically, the invention must be made available to the public on "reasonable terms." 35 U.S.C. § 201(f) (2009). For a contrary view regarding the scope of the phrase "reasonable term", *see* McCabe, *supra* note 37, at 664.
142 *See* Rai and Eisenberg, *supra* note 73, at 311. Rai and Eisenberg further submit proposals which enhance the use of march-in and the ease at which an agency can assert its rights without fear of violating the BDA. These proposals will be discussed later in this section.
143 *See* 35 U.S.C. § 203(a)(2) (2009). An example of support is shown in Mary Eberle's analysis of the CellPro petition decision. *See* Mary Eberle, *March-In Rights Under the Bayh-Dole Act: Public Access to Federally Funded Research,* 3 Marq. Intell. Prop. L. Rev. 155, 179 (1999) (stating that it appears a public health need indeed would not have been met but for the CellPro product).
144 Eberle, *supra* note 143, at 178.

3. Perceived Weaknesses and Asserted Ineffectiveness of the March-In Provision

Critics of the provision either assert that the idea of march-in has "chilling effects" on technology transfer, or note that its persistent nonuse over the past quarter-century has rendered it ineffective and unnecessary.[145]

a) March-In has Negative Effects on Technology Transfer

The GAO outlines four issues with the existence of the march-in right. First, there could be a "chilling effect" where an action may deter investors from investing in the commercialization, and some researchers from participating in the participating in federal research efforts.[146] Agency officials note that investors "are looking for profitable technologies and inventions that either have, or are close to obtaining a patent."[147] The march-in possibility could lead to uncertainty with respect to ownership of the invention, as well as a decrease in the perceived value of the investment.[148]

The second issue inherent in the march-in scheme is that the process as-is tends to be lengthy and will become unworkable in time-critical situations.[149] Even those supporting the use of march-in provisions note that the system should be amended to ensure that march-in can become effective in situations regarding life-saving drugs and other emergent issues.[150]

The GAO further finds that commercial products based on federal inventions often have multiple patents, some of which are not federally funded.[151] This presents a conflict because march-in will often involve, in effect, an end-product, and not an initial patent. By marching in, the government may not only be asserting the rights inherent in Bayh-Dole, but it may negatively affect another inventor whose invention was not part of the Bayh-Dole funding scheme.[152]

145 "Four key disincentives inhibit federal agencies use of Bayh-Dole march-in authority." GAO Report, *supra* note 68, at 12.

146 *See* GAO Report, *supra* note 68, at 12.

147 *Id.* at 13.

148 *See id.*

149 *See id.* at 12.

150 *See* Rai and Eisenberg, *supra* note 73, at 311. "Indeed, the tolerance for protracted delays inherent in the current process is at odds with the time-sensitive nature of the interests reflected." *Id.*

151 *See* GAO Report, *supra* note 68 , at 12.

152 It is notable that federal agencies may only have the authority to march in on one aspect of the product. However, this will complicate the procedure, rendering the march-in provision inefficient at best. Also, even if this is worked effectively, it may still negatively affect the value of all other patented inventions associated with the marched-in end-product. *See id.* at 14.

The GAO finally advises that the commercialization of an invention may be jeopardized if a licensee with specialized knowledge loses the knowledge subsequent to a march-in.[153] If an agency forces a contractor to license to someone subsequent to a march-in, the contractor would have to "consider whether the other patented technologies would be available to the new licensee and whether the new licensee would have the knowledge, resources, and commitment needed to commercialize the product."[154]

b) Nonuse of the Provision has Rendered it Unnecessary

A contingent of scholars have taken the stance that because the march-in provision has never been used, it is an unnecessary provision of the BDA.[155] Kevin McCabe analyzes the NIH's decision in CellPro and determines that economic theory suggests that "the Government will never initiate a march-in proceeding against a biotechnology company."[156] He explains that rational actors seek to maximize their investment return, and the government will rarely need to force a company to "take effective steps to achieve practical application."[157] McCabe also notes that investors, who are generally risk averse, would be "less willing to invest in biotechnology if the threat of government march-in ever became a reality."[158]

March-in has further been criticized as ineffective in serving the legislators' original goal to limit "the dark side of granting proprietary rights in publicly-funded technology," specifically the potential for contractors to take advantage of the Act without allowing the public to reap the fruits of an invention.[159] By explicitly rejecting four march-in petitions, it has been argued that the NIH is rejecting Congress's concerns that led it to coin the march-in provision.[160]

153 *See id.* at 12.
154 Thus, even if the license happened, it may hamper commercialization of an invention. *Id.* at 14.
155 *See* McCabe, *supra* note 37, at 661.
156 *Id.* Though McCabe's article specifically analyzes biotechnology, it can be inferred to relate to all aspects of technology transfer. To date, the only *petitions* ever filed for march-in were to the NIH, on biotechnological products. Thus, it seems that if the Government would ever use its march-in right, that biotechnology would be the likely industry of the invention. *See id.*
157 *Id.* In other words, no company would refuse to commercialize a product when it is in their best interest.
158 *Id.* This partially conflicts with the rationale of some agency representatives and scholars advocating for march-in under the theory that involved parties fear march-in, which drives the contractor to license to an investor. *See* GAO Report, *supra* note 68, at 11; *See* McGarey, *supra* note 108, at 1116.
159 Conley, *supra* note 66.
160 *See id.*

4. Evaluating the March-in Provision

a) Analysis

It is fairly certain that a correctly drafted and enforced provision regarding march-in would have a positive effect on the public without severely negatively affecting technology transfer.[161] Increasing access to technological products will increase the public good. However, the current march-in provision as drafted and enforced is entirely ineffective. The fact that the provision has never been used is *per se* evidence of its failure in the marketplace.

The arguments that march-in rights amount to a "scare tactic" and incentivize universities and other contractors to license their technology are unconvincing. Instead, I agree with the contention that the market forces are the true incentives behind technology transfer.[162]

Currently, the march-in right can only be used as a true "last resort." The government contractor must exhaust all court appeals before march-in can be granted.[163] This requirement will effectively continue to limit the number of march-in petitions that an entity will serve the government, and also will be crippling to the government if it ever wants to exercise its right.

b) Recommendations for Change

For the march-in right to become effective, it needs to be easy for the government to utilize, and it needs to embrace instead of conflict with the "economic theory" arguments that McCabe presented.[164]

The march-in procedure is covered in 37 C.F.R. § 401.6.[165] The agency can initiate a proceeding "whenever it receives information that it believes might warrant the exercise of march-in rights."[166] This shows that the agency has full power to initiate march-in, even without a petition from another party. Hence, the law governing exercise of march-in is not constricting in itself; the interpretations and fears of the government need to be relaxed to ensure an effective procedure.

161 *See* Eberle, *supra* note 144, at 179.
162 *See generally* McCabe, *supra* note 37, at 661.
163 *See* Rai and Eisenberg, *supra* note 73, at 311.
164 *See* McCabe, *supra* note 37, at 661-662; *See* Chapter IV-A-3-b, *infra.*
165 *See* 37 C.F.R. § 401.6 (2006).
166 John H. Raubitschek and Norman J. Latker, *Reasonable Pricing – A New Twist for March-In Rights Under the Bayh-Dole Act*, 22 SANTA CLARA COMPUTER & HIGH TECH L.J. 149, 156 (2005).

As a preliminary matter, investors must see the possibility of march-in as something that would not limit the value in a given investment. To achieve this, one must more explicitly state conditions that will bring about march-in. Currently, "there is very little legislative history on march-in rights and nothing relating to when they are to be used."[167] The statute explains four conditions for march-in, but the provisions fail to adequately describe circumstances that justify the march-in.[168] By more explicitly defining the issues that could result in march-in, the ensuring transparency will allow investors to more easily determine the potential of their investment being undermined. This, in turn, will allay the fears of the government agency wishing execute a march-in.

Raubitschek and Latker note that a university currently only has to take "effective steps" to achieve commercialization.[169] Arno and Davis note that the agencies continually fail to acknowledge that failure to offer reasonable prices are grounds for a march-in.[170] While this requirement is not expressly written in the BDA, it reconciles with many of its the policy goals. By amending or redefining the march-in provision to be enforceable in the event of unreasonable pricing offered by a university, the march-in provision will become much more easily usable, benefit the public, and not scare investors since the standard for reasonable pricing shall be explicit and prices charged by contractors will be transparent.

Rai and Eisenberg further note that the contractor should not have to "exhaust all court appeals" before march-in can be authorized.[171] This would be a relatively simple solution to allow for march-in to become efficient and effective instead of burdensome and time consuming.

Though there are numerous criticisms of a strong march-in, it is important to note that the above modifications will not harm technology transfer. Eberle notes that forced licensing may generate uncertainty, but companies will not "turn their backs" on university technology.[172] Furthermore, Halperin notes that without having march-in rights consistently enforced, government contractors "will understand that they can obtain on the cheap tremendous benefits from taxpayer-funded research and then, without risk of sanction, turn around and charge the same taxpayers highly-inflated monopoly prices."[173] By more clearly defining the grounds for march-in and adding "reasonable prices" to the statute, government agencies will

167 *Id.* at 162.
168 *See* 25 U.S.C. § 203(a)(1-2) (2009).
169 The university does not have to achieve practical application. Raubitschek, *supra* note 166, at 160-61.
170 *See* Arno and Davis, *supra* note , at 666. This view is criticized by Raubitschek. Raubitschek, *supra* note 166, at 160 (noting that there is no explicit reasonable pricing requirement in the Act).
171 Rai and Eisenberg, *supra* note 73, at 311.
172 Eberle, *supra* note 144 at 178.
173 Halperin, *supra* note 112, at 17.

have less fear in utilizing their rights, and the transparency of the provision will ensure that technology transfer is not chilled.

B. *Is Bayh-Dole's Shift in Presumption of Ownership Effective? A Review of Empirical Data*

This section undertakes to determine whether or not the policies advocated by Bayh-Dole under § 200 have been accomplished pursuant to the general provisions disposing rights to a contractor under § 202. The effect of the ability for a contractor to retain ownership, and by extension, the Act as a whole, will be analyzed based upon three criteria:

1) Has Bayh-Dole led to an increase in patenting, and if so, are these patents "important," and is the increase beneficial to the public?
2) Has Bayh-Dole led to an increase in commercialization of inventions, and if so, has increased commercialism benefitted the marketplace?
3) Has Bayh-Dole advanced or retarded scientific progress, and what is the effect on the U.S. economy?

1. Bayh-Dole's Effect on Patenting

Some general conclusions with regards to the BDA's effect on patenting can be made using evidence of the number of patents in a university portfolio before and after Bayh-Dole. At first glance, the uptick in number of patents granted to U.S. research universities seems to be directly related to the time period of the Bayh-Dole Act's enactment (see Appendix A – Figure 1).[174] As seen from the figure, the number of patents stayed fairly steady and minimal until 1970, and increased slowly between 1970 and 1980. After the BDA's passage, the number of granted patents nearly doubled between 1980-1985, then increased more than twofold between 1985-1990, and again nearly doubled between 1990-1995. Proponents of the Act's success point to this easily quantifiable trend as *per se* evidence of Bayh-Dole's success.[175]

174 *See* David Roessner et al., *The Economic Impact of Licensed Commercialized Inventions Originating in University Research, 1996-200,* Final Report to the Biotechnology Industry Organization (September 3, 2009), *hereinafter* Economics Report, at page 15 (reproduced in Appendix A: Figure 1).

175 *See generally* Howard Bremer et al., *The Bayh-Dole Act and Revisionism Redux,* at page 6, Life Sciences Law & Industry, Vol. 3, No. 17 (September 11, 2009).

a) Importance and Generality

BDA detractors argue both that the increase in the number of patents is due to factors outside of Bayh-Dole, and also that it is not necessarily a benefit to technology transfer.[176] Specifically, two studies[177] attempt to show that even though Bayh-Dole led to an increase of the patents, they are not "important" and lack generality.[178] Henderson, Jaffe, and Trajtenberg undertook to prove this by determining the frequency with which patents were cited in subsequent research.[179]

To test the Henderson evidence, Mowery charts the amount of "citations"[180] based on patents in both biomedical and nonbiomedical inventions.[181] Mowery points to little increase in citation percentages post-Bayh-Dole, and concludes, to an extent, that the general increase in patents generally did not result in "better" inventions.[182] However, Mowery's research contradicted the Henderson findings as it did not show any decline of importance of patents post-Bayh-Dole based upon citation level.

To better reconcile these two studies, a practical method to determine whether or not Bayh-Dole is having a "useful" effect on technology transfer is to see how

176 *See* Mowery, *supra* note 5, at 126; *See* Chapter III-B-1, *supra*.

177 *See* Rebecca Henderson, Adam Jaffe, and Manuel Trajtenberg, *Universities as a Source of Commercial Technology: A Detailed Analysis of University Patenting, 1965-1988,* at page 123, (President and Fellows of Harvard College and the Massachusetts Institute of Technology, 1998), *available at* http://www.tau.ac.il/~manuel/pdfs/univeristies_as_a_source.pdf; *see* Mowery, *supra* note 5 , at 119.

178 *See* Henderson, Jaffe and Trajtenberg, supra note 178, at 122-23. Henderson's study defines "importance" by a statistical formula summing the number of instances reference to a patent is cited and reducing them by a discount factor. This is because "at least some of such future inventions will reference or cite the original invention in their patents, thereby making the number and character of citations received a valid indicator of the technological importance of an invention" *Id.* at 122. Furthermore, generality is characterized by an exponential summation function with citations as a variable, with the net effect of indicating the "basicness" of the research. *Id.* at 123. The researchers create this variable pursuant to their hypothesis that "patents that cover more ''basic'' research will be cited by work in a broader range of fields" *Id.*

179 *See id.* at 123. The findings of the researchers supported the hypothesis that the importance and generality of inventions declined post-Bayh-Dole in a fairly robust fashion. *Id.* at 124.

180 *See* Mowery, *supra* note 5, at 119. Mowery defines a "citation" as "the number of citations received by each patent following its issue" for six years. He notes that this is a good variable to measure importance of a patent, assuming "citations form an index of the influence over subsequent inventive activity of the cited patent." Mowery qualifies his analysis by stating that recent patents will be underrepresented, because many patents take 4-5 years for citations to peak. *Id.*

181 *See id.* at 113-125 (including tables 6.4, 6.5, and 6.6).

182 Mowery's statistics showed little effect (positive or negative) regarding the 'generality' and 'importance' of post Bayh-Dole patents compared to pre-Bayh-Dole. This finding invalidated his original hypothesis, based on the Henderson study, that importance and generality would decline in patents post-Bayh-Dole. *See id.* at 125-26, 148.

commercialization of patents has been shaped post-Bayh Dole. This will be presented in section IV-B-2, *infra.*

b) Rise in Biotechnological Patents

With regards to "important" inventions in the biotechnology fields, it is fairly clear that Bayh-Dole led to the creation of numerous FDA approved drugs. In the years immediately following 1980, the amount of drugs created with public funding increased immensely.[183]

Mowery attempts to discredit Bayh-Dole as the driving factor for the rise in these important biotechnological inventions. By noting the same level of increase in biomedical patents versus nonbiomedical patents after the BDA, Mowery attempts to formulate the argument that Bayh-Dole was not the driving factor of the biotech revolution, and, by proxy, of the increase in patents in general.[184]

In response to the critics, one can hypothesize that the uptick in biotechnology and patenting in general was, in part, fostered by Bayh-Dole. While it is clear that the percentage of biotechnical inventions did rise before the act, several factors related to Bayh-Dole instigated this rise. The IPA system enacted in 1968 enabled universities to manage their own inventions made with NIH (and later NSF) support.[185] Thus, though critics[186] point to the rise in biotech before 1980 as a reason that Bayh-Dole was an effect rather than a cause of increased patenting, this argument fails to consider the effects of Bayh-Dole provisions before the actual passing of the Act.

Similarly, patenting of biotechnological inventions increased because of the shift in incentives offered by Bayh-Dole. While critics contend that Bayh-Dole did not contribute to the rise in biotechnological patenting, they fail to acknowledge the reliance the biotechnology field places on patenting;[187] the ease with which the university can assert rights over its invention because of Bayh-Dole led to the ability to patent biotech inventions early and often. This can be substantiated by the fact that after 1980 there "was a dramatic rise in the propensity to patent on the part of

183 *See* Vickie Loise and Ashley Stevens, *The Bayh-Dole Act Turns 30,* les Nouvelles 185, at 190 (December 2010) (at figure 2).

184 *See* Mowery, supra note 5, at 126-27.

185 *See* Bremer, *supra* note 175 , at 3-5. The IPA, or Institutional Patent Agreement system was the clear precursor of the Bayh-Dole Act. It allowed universities to manage their own inventions, but became undermined in future years. The desire for the "IPA program be made statutory and binding on all federal agencies, and that it be extended to small business contractors" led to the drafting of the Bayh-Dole Act.

186 *See* David C. Mowery et al., *The growth of patenting and licensing by U.S. universities: an assessment of the effects of the Bayh-Dole act of 1980,* 30 RES. POL. (ELSEVIER) 99, 104 (2001).

187 *See* Burrone, *supra* note 84.

universities that had never applied for patents before and that universities that had always patented began to do so more intensely."[188]

c) Anticommons Concerns

While some Bayh-Dole opponents admit that the Act had a positive effect on patenting, especially in biotechnology, they advance the argument that the rise in patenting will lead to an anticommons concern and deter innovation in the long run.[189] Two potential routes to an anticommons issue exist, one being "creating too many concurrent fragments of intellectual property rights in potential future products" and the other being "permitting too many upstream patent owners to stack licenses on top of the future discoveries of downstream users."[190] Both examples are potentially exacerbated by the presence of Bayh-Dole, where early-stage patenting is encouraged and the ability to grant many nonexclusive licenses is incentivized.

The real-world effects of an anticommons scenario would be a reduction in use, commercialization, and further research and development of inventions. Empirical evidence points against the anticommons concern being prevalent today, even in the biotech industry, where upstream patenting occurs frequently. The next section produces evidence in support of this contention.

2. Bayh-Dole's Effect on Commercialization

Whether or not the BDA has achieved its policy objective of "promot[ing] the commercialization and public availability of inventions" is a major factor in determining the success of the Act.[191] An increase in commercialization would effectively refute the hypothesis that the BDA creates an anticommons effect.[192]

Economists at the Max Planck Institute for Economics have undertaken to determine how technology is being transferred, and what factors affect the flow of

188 Charles R. McManis and Sucheol Noh, THE IMPACT OF THE BAYH-DOLE ACT ON GENETIC RESEARCH AND DEVELOPMENT: EVALUATING THE ARGUMENTS AND EMPIRICAL EVIDENCE TO DATE 13, *available at* papers.ssrn.com/sol3/papers.cfm?abstract_id=1840639.

189 *See, e.g.* Heller and Eisenberg, *supra* note 103.

190 *Id.* at 699.

191 35 U.S.C. § 200 (2009).

192 By showing an increase in commercialization, it would be clear that the resource at issue (the patent) is not being underused. *See* Chapter IV-B-1, *supra.*

knowledge and invention.[193] The economists used statistical models which can be summarized by the forthcoming results.

As a preliminary issue, the researchers found that the likelihood that an invention is successfully licensed is enhanced by the presence and scope of patents related to the invention.[194] This finding refutes the anticommons concern of Bayh-Dole critics.[195]

With respect to other related issues of commercialization, the economists' findings were not so clear. For example, the researchers could not confirm their hypothesis that "academic inventions from collaborative research with industry partners are more likely to be licensed than other inventions" and reject the hypothesis that "spin-off licensees significantly differ from external licensees in their likelihood to commercialize inventions or in the level of royalties."[196] Thus, even though data shows Bayh-Dole has led to an increase in collaborative work and creation of startups, the evidence questions the effects of this on technology transfer.[197]

Despite the potential shortfalls noted in the Max Planck study, statistics show that commercialization has been widespread since Bayh-Dole. University research created 1.32 products, on average, per day, from fiscal year 2006.[198] This success is unique to the United States and vastly greater than the amount prior to Bayh-Dole. Even more notably, there were nearly 5,000 existing university licenses in 2006, which shows clear evidence of the university-industry partnership that Bayh-Dole has fostered.[199] Numerous universities point to Bayh-Dole as the driving factor behind the development and commercialization of life-saving drugs.[200] Despite critiques from opponents of the Act, the BDA's effects on commercialization are clear and positive.

3. Bayh-Dole's Effect on Research and Scientific Progress

As previously noted, critics argue that a weakness of the BDA is that it shifts the focus from basic to applied research, and that it creates conflicts of interests in

193 *See* Guido Buenstorf and Matthias Geissler, *Not invented here: Technology licensing, knowledge transfer and innovation based on public* research, Papers on Economics and Evolution, Max-Planck-Gesellschaft (December, 2009).

194 This is true for both domestic and foreign licensees. *See id.* at section 6.1.

195 While Bayh-Dole does promote patenting, patented inventions are more likely to be licensed, which inevitably results in commercial use and future development. *See id.*

196 *Id.* at section 6.2 (hypothesis 2a and 5).

197 For statistics regarding startups, see footnote 77, *supra.*

198 *See* Bremer et al., *supra* note 175, at 9.

199 *See id.*

200 *See* Emory Press Release, *supra* note 3 ; *see* Bremer et al., *supra* note 175 , at 9.

researchers who may be more likely to withhold their research for fear that a university will gain patent rights.[201]

McManis and Noh attempt to determine whether or not Bayh-Dole has generated any inefficiencies on its own that lead the university research and development world to be less productive than it would absent the scheme. With regards to dissemination of research, they found that though there is "some evidence suggesting increasing secrecy and delays in the dissemination of genetic research, it is not at all clear that the concomitant increase in university patenting and licensing necessarily bears any causal relation."[202] With respect to diversion of research, the authors cite a Thursby and Thursby study finding that there have been some changes in the direction of faculty research, but "much of the available evidence suggests that faculty have not been diverted from their traditional role in the creation of knowledge."[203] Other academics similarly note that there is no evidence that research "has become any less fundamental" after Bayh-Dole.[204] The evidence and lack of contrary evidence all point to the conclusion that Bayh-Dole is no more inefficient with respect to promoting academic research than the pre Bayh-Dole scheme.

The next chapters look into the future of Bayh-Dole. Chapter V examines the recent *Stanford* case, which may exacerbate some related concerns with respect to the force, interpretation, and application of the BDA. Chapter VI will assess the evidence presented and determine how Bayh-Dole provisions can be effective overseas, despite noted differences in university technology transfer systems.

201 *See* Chapter III, *supra*.
202 McManis and Noh, *supra* note 188, at 26.
203 *Id.* at 27, *citing* Jerry G. Thursby and Marie C. Thursby, University Licensing Under Bayh-Dole: What are the Issues and Evidence?" (May 2003.).
204 Richard R. Nelson, *Observations on the Post-Bayh-Dole Rise of Patenting at American Universities*, 26 J. TECH. TRANSFER 13, 14 (2001).

V. Bayh-Dole Moving Forward: Ownership Concerns and the Stanford v Roche Case

Behind all of its policy objectives, extra provisions, and exceptional circumstances, the main change Bayh-Dole provides the university technology transfer scene is clear: the presumption of ownership has shifted from the government to the university. The results are positive: the government did not see to it that inventions under their funding were further developed and commercialized pre-Bayh-Dole.[205] Now, empirical evidence shows that post Bayh-Dole, universities are commercializing.[206]

Though Bayh-Dole has been shown to incentivize technology transfer, whether it does so in the most efficient manner is questionable. At the heart of the matter is whether Bayh-Dole places ownership in the hands of the correct body, and how courts will interpret the ownership provisions.

A. Who Develops a University Invention?

It seems to be a reasonable conclusion that legislation should favor the patent law principle that ownership of a patent should rest in the hands of its true inventor.[207] A study from Robert Lowe addresses how a university invention is developed.[208]

Through a series of statistical formulas, Lowe concludes that "inventions associated with high levels of tacit knowledge" should allow for the inventor to "extract full monopoly rents related to the invention."[209] However, in inventions requiring "less than full effort," "university policies requiring a royalty rate distort final output and result in a transfer from inventor to university with no apparent added productivity."[210] This inefficiency hints at the dilemma the Supreme Court recently faced in determining whether or not Bayh-Dole automatically vests ownership in

205 *See* Bremer et al., *supra* note 175.

206 For evidence of this, *see* Section IV-B-2, *supra.*

207 "The general rule is that... patent rights... belong to the creator of the property." Ernest I. Gifford, WHO'S THE OWNER? *Michigan Bar Journal* 21-23 (Aug, 2004).

208 *See* Robert A. Lowe, *Who Develops a University Invention? The Impact of Tacit Knowledge and Licensing Policies*, 31 J. TECH. TRANSFER (Netherlands) 415, 415 (2006).

209 *Id.* at 426.

210 *Id.* at 427.

the university, or whether it initially remains with the inventor absent an assignment.

B. The Stanford v. Roche Case

1. The Legal Issue

§ 202 of the BDA states that "each nonprofit organization or small business firm may, within a reasonable time after disclosure as required by paragraph (c) (1) of this section, elect to retain title to any subject invention."[211] In *Stanford,* the question arose as to whether or not this provision implied that title in an invention automatically vested in the nonprofit or small business, and not in the inventor himself.

2. The Facts

The facts behind the *Stanford* case reinforce the claim that complicated fact sequences often give rise to major legal conundrums.[212] In 1985 Cetus, a small California company, began to develop methods to quantify levels of the human immunodeficiency virus (HIV).[213] The situation involved three patents regarding AIDS monitoring.[214] One of the named inventors, Mark Holodniy, was a researcher at Stanford in 1988.

In 1988, Holodniy became a research fellow at Stanford and signed a "Copyright and Patent Agreement" that obligated him to assign his inventions to the university.[215] However, in early 1989, Holodniy would visit Cetus to learn techniques related to his field.[216] In exchange for the education received, Holodniy signed a contract that stated he "will assign and do[es] hereby assign to CETUS, my right, title, and interest in each of the ideas, inventions and improvements... as a consequence of" his work at Cetus.[217]

211 35 U.S.C. § 202 (a) (2009).

212 *See* Sanjesh Sharma, *The Bayh-Dole Act and Allocation of Ownership Rights in Inventions Arising out of Federally Funded Research,* 8 INTELL. PROP. & TECH. L.J. 23, 23 (August, 2011).

213 *See* Stanford, *supra* note 10, at 1-2.

214 *See* Board of Trustees of the Leland Stanford Junior University v. Roche Molecular Systems, Inc. 583 F.3d 832, 837 (Fed. Cir, 2008), *aff'd* 563 U.S. ____ (2011) (*hereinafter* Stanford(CAFC)).

215 Stanford(CAFC), *supra* note 214, at 837.

216 *Id.*

217 *Id.*

Holodniy ultimately produced an assay to measure the amount of plasma HIV in samples from infected humans.[218] Holodniy and the other named inventors completed this work while at Stanford University. Stanford's HIV research was partially funded by the NIH, which is a federal agency. This allowed Stanford to claim its right to retain ownership under the Bayh-Dole Act.

Roche purchased Cetus' business in 1991 and subsequently began manufacturing HIV detection kits with the Holodniy assays. In May, 1992, Stanford filed a patent application, and the relevant patents were granted years later.

Stanford invoked Bayh-Dole in formally announcing to the government that it elected to retain title to the inventions under the Act.[219] Stanford filed suit in October of 2005, asserting that Roche's HIV detection kits infringed the patents.[220]Roche counterclaimed against Stanford and the named inventors, asserting "that Stanford lacked standing against Roche, and that Roche possesses ownership, license, and/or shop rights to the patents through Roche's acquisition of Cetus' PCR assets...."[221] Roche's basis for the challenge on standing was that Holodniy's assignment to Cetus was valid, and that Stanford's rights under Bayh-Dole could not trump the original contract between Cetus and Holodniy.

3. The Proceedings

a) The Federal Circuit Opinion

The Northern District of California found for Stanford and Roche subsequently appealed to the Federal Circuit. The Federal Circuit stated that the challenge of Stanford's ownership is a valid challenge and defense to infringement.[222]

The Federal Circuit noted that the issue of whether contractual language effects a present assignment of patent rights or an agreement to assign rights in the future is to be resolved at the federal level.[223] Thus, the court examined the contract between Stanford and Holodniy in detail, noting that the agreement states that Holodniy would "agree to assign or confirm in writing..." his interests in the particular invention.[224] The court analyzed the words "agree to assign" as a promise to assign rights in the future, and not an immediate transfer of the interest.[225]

218 *See id.*.
219 *Id. at* 838.
220 *See id.*
221 *See id.*
222 *See id.* at 839.
223 *See id.* at 841.
224 *Id.*
225 *See id.*

The court next undertook to examine Holodniy's contract with Cetus. The Cetus contract specifically used the wording "I will assign and hereby do assign... my right... in each of the ideas, inventions, and improvements."[226] The Federal Circuit determined that this contract *does* contain an implicit transfer of interests, and that Cetus immediately gained equitable title to the invention.[227] The Federal Circuit used its reasoning in *FilmTec* to determine that the language of the Stanford assignment was a future assignment, and the language of the Cetus assignment was a present assignment.[228]

Stanford next argued that even if the Stanford contract did not automatically transfer Holodniy's interest to the university, the Bayh-Dole Act contemplates that Stanford should automatically obtain ownership of the patent, and thus Holodniy would have had no right in the patent to assign to Cetus.[229] The Federal Circuit reversed the District Court in this regard, and stated that the BDA could not automatically void Holodniy's assignment to Cetus, and it, at most, provided the government with a discretionary option to his rights.[230]

Stanford argued that § 202(d) of the Bayh-Dole Act states that Holodniy could only keep title to his inventions "if a contractor does not elect to retain title to a subject invention."[231] The court dismisses this argument by stating that "the primary purpose of the Bayh-Dole Act is to regulate relationships of small business and nonprofit grantees with the government, not between grantees and the inventors who work for them."[232]

226 *Id* at 842.

227 *See id.*

228 *See generally* Filmtec Corporation v. Allied-Signal Inc., 939 F.2d 1568, 1572 (Fed. Cir. 1991).

229 *See generally* Stanford(CAFC), *supra* note 214, at 844-45.

230 *See id.* at 844.

231 *Id.*, *citing* 35 USC § 202(d). The provision states that "if a contractor does not elect to retain title to a subject invention, the Federal agency may consider... grant requests for retention of rights by the inventor. " The court determines that this provision does *not* mean that the contractor automatically gains rights to an invention if government funding is involved; the Act "does not automatically void ab initio the inventors' rights in government-funded inventions." *See id* at 844, *citing* Central Admixture Pharmacy Services, Inc. v. Advanced Cardiac Solutions, P.C., 482 F.3d 1347, 1352-53.

232 *See id.*, at 845; *see* Fenn v. Yale Univ., 393 F. Supp. 2d 133, 141-4 (D. Conn. 2004). In *Fenn*, the court reaffirmed the fact that the Bayh-Dole Act was designed to "support federally funded research and to regulate relationships between the federal Government and its small business and nonprofit contractors.".

b) The Supreme Court Decision

SCOTUS granted certiorari to determine whether or not Bayh-Dole "flipped" the general rule that patent rights first vest with the inventor.[233] Though SCOTUS in recent years has tended only to hear patent-related Federal Circuit cases when it feels that the Federal Circuit erred, the majority fully agreed with the Federal Circuit's interpretation of the law and noted that Bayh-Dole should not override fundamental principles of patent law.

Chief Justice Roberts stated that the BDA was passed to "promote the utilization of innovations arising from federally supported research," promote collaboration between commercial concerns and nonprofit organizations," and "ensure that the Government obtains sufficient rights in federally supported inventions.[234]

The court notes that the ability for contractors to retain title is not automatic. If obligations are not satisfied, the government may receive title under § 202 and § 203.[235]

The court announces that the government retaining some rights to the invention should not preclude the original inventor from asserting his own rights. Specifically, precedent confirms the "general rule that rights in an invention belong to the inventor" and that "an inventor can assign his rights in an invention to the third party."[236] Therefore, the court concludes that "unless there is an agreement to the contrary, an employer does not have rights in an invention which is the original conception of the employee alone.[237]

With regard to the argument that the BDA actually "reorders the normal priority in an invention," the court notes that Congress has stripped inventors of rights in their inventions in certain situations by using express language, for example with respect to some contracts dealing with nuclear material. Under the BDA, there is no express language to divest the original investors of their rights.[238]

The court finally concludes that the Bayh-Dole provision that contractors may elect to retain title confirms that the BDA does not automatically vest the title.[239] Chief Justice Roberts states that "the Act's disposition of rights... serves to clarify

233 *See* "Supreme Court to hear Bayh-Dole Patent Ownership Dispute: Stanford v. Roche", Patently-O: The nation's leading patent law blog, *available at* http://www.patentlyo.com/patent/2010/11/supreme-court-to-hear-bayh-dole-patent-ownership- dispute-stanford-v-roche.html (Nov 01, 2010).

234 Stanford, *supra* note 10 , at 3, *citing* 35 U.S.C. § 200 (2009).

235 *See id.* If the Government utilizes § 203 to march-in, it gains title to the extent that it can require anyone with interest in the subject invention to grant a license to a reasonable applicant, as well as to the extent that the Government can grant a license itself if it is reasonable under the circumstances. *See* 35 U.S.C. § 203 (2009).

236 Stanford, *supra* note 10, at 7.

237 *Id.* at 7, *citing* United States v. Dubilier Condenser Corp., 289 U.S. 178, 187 (1933).

238 *See id.* at 8.

239 *See id.* at 11.

the order of priority of rights between the Federal Government and a federal contractor in a federally funded invention that already belongs to the contractor. Nothing more."[240] With this in mind, the court affirmed the Federal Circuit opinion upholding Roche's challenge to Stanford's ownership.

4. Future Implications

While the ramifications of the decision will not be known for some time, the case brings to light some issues that may result in the university technology transfer sector. The difficulty facing the Supreme Court is apparent based upon the dichotomy between Bayh-Dole and patent law: the decision not to override patent law has been criticized as being "inconsistent with the [Bayh-Dole] Act's basic purposes," thus undercutting the Act's ability to encourage innovation and technology transfer.[241] However, the decision has been hailed by supporters as ensuring that the basic, justifiable principle that ownership of an invention should be afforded to the inventor still exists despite the Bayh-Dole Act.[242] If Bayh-Dole was interpreted to supersede this principle, the implications for technology transfer could become more severe if inventors became less willing to innovate since a university employer would automatically gain ownership in their work. Though scholars and practitioners alike differ on their opinions of the decision, it is unanimous among them that the decision is a limitation of the Bayh-Dole Act and may carry lasting effects on the government contractors, specifically universities, and especially with regards to technology transfer.

a) Implications with Respect to Contract Drafting

It is fairly clear from the language in both the Federal Circuit and SCOTUS opinions that the entire issue could have been avoided had Stanford used airtight language in its assignment contract with Holodniy. General patent law ownership principles do not conflict with contract law, and an inventor can freely transfer his rights to an employer via contract. If Stanford's contract ensured immediate transfer of rights from Holodniy's inventions, Stanford would have title, and could invoke the Bayh-Dole Act to retain ownership from the Government. Holodniy's transfer to Cetus

240 *Id.* at 12.

241 *See* Stanford v. Roche, Bayh-Dole and the Intersection of Patent and Tax Exemption, Nonprofit Law Prof Blog, http://lawprofessors.typepad.com/nonprofit/2011/06/stanford-v-roche-bayh-dole-and-the-intersection-of-patent-and-tax-exemption.html (June 21, 2011).

242 *See* Gifford, *supra* note 207.

would have likely been found void.[243] In oral arguments, Justice Ginsburg pointed out that the "whole thing that was wrong here is that Stanford, instead of drafting the agreements as 'I agree to assign,' should have said 'I hereby assign,' and then there would be no case.[244]

The Federal Circuit originally decided the case based upon the language of the Stanford assignment being one relating to future and not immediate transfer.[245] The literal consequence of such a decision is simple and straightforward: universities and other enterprises will be much more vigilant in creating assignment contracts with their employees.

A New York Times article notes that despite the fact that the case essentially hinged on the wording of the Stanford contract, the implications will be broader.[246] One feasible effect of the case is that it will change the relationship between universities and their faculties. The article promotes the fact that the relationship is likely to become "more legalistic and more mercantile."[247] Ultimately, the article maintains that Bayh-Dole's principles have been ignored, and collaborative enterprising will be minimized as a result of this decision.[248] In contrast to the success Bayh-Dole has brought the U.S., the Stanford decision may serve to stymie such innovation.

b) Gap in the Law between Patent Rights and Bayh-Dole Obligations

In his opinion, Chief Justice Roberts specifically states that if Congress wanted Bayh-Dole to "intend such a sea change in intellectual property, it would have done so clearly."[249] Roberts concludes that the BDA does not override the centuries-old

243 The Supreme Court did not conclusively determine whether or not, if Stanford's contract adequately produced a present assignment of a future interest similar to Cetus's contract, Bayh-Dole could be invoked to ensure the institution captures the full interest instead of the competing right-holder. Justice Sotamayor's concurrence seems to consider this question ripe for a future case. *See* Jonathan T. Cain et al., Invention Assignment Following *Stanford v. Roche:* Implications for Technology Transfer and Government Contracts, *published by* LexisNexis Martindale-Hubbell, June 30, 2011.

244 Alex Philippidis, *Stanford v. Roche* Could Place Tech Transfer on Shaky Ground, Genetic Engineering & Biotechnology News, Mar 17, 2011, *available at* http://www.genengnews.com/analysis-and-insight/i-stanford-v-roche-i-could-place-tech-transfer-on-shaky-ground/77899372/.

245 *See generally* Andrew H. Berks, Stanford v. Roche – When is an assignment not an assignment?, http://berksiplaw.com/2011/06/stanford-v-roche/ (June 12, 2011).

246 *See* Op-Ed., *The Fair Rewards of Invention,* N.Y. Times, June 7, 2011, *reprinted at* http://www.nytimes.com/2011/06/08/opinion/08wed3.html?_r=1.

247 *Id.*

248 *See id.*

249 Robert Barnes, *Supreme Court limits patent rights of university* research, Wash. Post, June 7, 2011, *available at* http://www.washingtonpost.com/politics/supreme-court-limits-patent-rights-of-university-research/2011/06/06/AG0UpbKH_story.html.

presumption that an inventor is the owner of his invention.[250] Unfortunately, by limiting the construction of the BDA to one that does not conflict with principles of patent ownership, Justice Roberts creates a gap that inherently undermines some of BDA's principles and provisions.

Cain et al note that the decision highlights a "gap in the law" between ownership of the invention and the duties levied on government funding recipients by the Act.[251] The Act specifically allows for the government to "march-in" and grant licenses under certain circumstances, all relating to the contractee's inadequate performance of certain requirements.[252]

The BDA does not specifically impose a duty on the contractor to ensure that it obtains ownership of the invention, yet the march-in provision grants the government rights that, under the *Stanford* rationale, only can be executed if the contractor *did* gain ownership of the invention. Therefore, failure to adequately gain control of the invention may lead to a tension between the contractor and the government, as the holding of the case implies that the government cannot maintain any march-in on an invention that it helped fund, so long as the inventor has not distinctly relinquished control of the invention to the contractor. This could complicate the front end of technology transfer, where the government may be less willing to engage in funding certain research.

Additionally, this decision may run contrary to the policy of the BDA that is highlighted by the prohibition of assignments.[253] Because the Act prohibits universities from assigning rights away from themselves, the expectation of the government as contemplated by the Act is that the university will have the rights to an invention in the first place. This holding shows that there are situations where a university is unable to procure rights, which seems to run counter to the entire purpose of the Bayh-Dole Act.This can be further substantiated by recognizing that "it would not make sense that the government would fund research and then not expect the university to own the patent." [254]

250 *See* Stanford, *supra* note 10, at 6.

251 Cain et al., *supra* note 243.

252 *See* 35 U.S.C. 203 (One of four situations must occur before the Government can assert its march-in right. *See* Chapter II, *infra*).

253 *See* 35 U.S.C. § 202(7)(a) (2009); *See* Chapter I-A-2, *supra.*

254 *Stanford v. Roche* decision requires extra care in managing university IP, The Tech Transfer Blog, http://www.technologytransfertactics.com/content/2011/07/13/stanford-v-roche-decision-requires-extra-care-in-managing-university-ip/ (July 13, 2011).

c) General Complications for the Technology Transfer Sector

It is possible that this case will make investors more wary of receiving licenses from universities given the chance that an invention may be licensed without proper title. If this possibility exists, an invention will be valued much more weakly. Critics of the decision note that university-researched patents would be less likely to pierce the market because no one "will be willing to take a risk on the patent."[255] Stanford argued that its technology transfer efforts will be damaged because a decision for Roche would add an additional inherent requirement of a Bayh-Dole entity to verify ownership of patent rights, which is very difficult in practice.[256]

Another concern includes the possibility of multiple parties believing that others may have ownership in an invention could lead to an anticommons issue of sorts. In a worst-case scenario, no one will feel an incentive to try and commercialize and the invention will be underused.

The effects of this case remain to be seen. In limiting Bayh-Dole's scope, the court rightfully protects what many believe to be the true inventor of a university invention. The court's holding is most consistent with the policy goals of patent law. Notwithstanding the fact that the opposite holding may have caused more troubles for university technology transfer, this decision does carry the possibility of introducing new complications for the sector. The final chapter serves to examine how Bayh-Dole, despite its flaws, could stimulate technology transfer in international jurisdictions.

255 Cain et al., *supra* note 243.
256 *See* Philippidis, *supra* note 244.

VI. Bayh-Dole Abroad: International Efforts to Emulate the Statute, and Recommendations for Future Success

Numerous developed countries have enacted or are considering enacting Bayh-Dole-like provisions.[257] Most notably, the Japanese Government in 1999 enacted a simple provision referred to as the "Japanese Bayh-Dole."[258] Several European countries have also enacted provisions to change the ownership presumptions of government funded technology transfer in the past decade.[259] With respect to developing countries, India is currently debating whether to enact its own version of a Bayh-Dole Act. The conflicting opinions in India and Europe underlie two major questions that countries around the world are attempting to solve: has Bayh-Dole truly worked in the United States, and if so, what are its chances of working in a given country?

A. Japan

The Japanese BDA, though very limited in scope, makes it possible for "private-sector corporations entrusted with R&D by the government to own the IP."[260] Thus, the Japanese Act includes a similar change in presumption of ownership to the US BDA.

Studies have shown that the shift in ownership has lead to increased commercialization in Japan, despite the lack of explicit provisions and policy goals similar to the United States Act.[261] A case study involving a research and development project in Japan notes that private contracts help support the Japanese provision, rendering the need for explicit provisions with regards to commercialization and duties moot.[262] While some critics of moving Bayh-Dole abroad point to the differences in structures of university systems between the U.S. and abroad, it is still noted that Japan is focused on encouraging technology transfer and benefits that

257 *See* Mireles, *supra* note 75, at 260.

258 *See* Ryoichi Namikawa, *Intellectual property in R&D project under Japanese Bayh-Dole system,* 9-1/2 Int. J. Technology Transfer and Commercialisation 9, 11 (2010).

259 *See* Mireles, *supra* note 75, at 270.

260 Namikawa, *supra* note 258 , at 11. Prior to this provision, all patent rights on inventions made with government funding were transferred to the government.

261 *See id.* "The Japanese Bayh-Dole Act is not supported by detailed rules, etc. but it has worked frequently and successfully." *Id.*

262 *Id.*

flow from the universities in its country.[263] A study in the nanotechnology field has noted that over the past ten years, the model for public to private transfer of technology has changed to a Bayh-Dole fostered scheme of universities to industry.[264] The success of this Act has shown that a Bayh-Dole-type statute can succeed to an extent in other developed countries, even if the university structure is not identical to that of the U.S.

B. Europe

European countries wishing to emulate the success of United States technology transfer have attempted to adapt statutes mimicking Bayh-Dole. Currently, Germany, the UK, France, Denmark, Austria, Norway Portugal, Spain and Finland either have or are considering legislation similar to the U.S. BDA.[265] Further, the Council of the European Union has noted that "the overall innovation environment of the EU remains weak in a number of key respects," especially with respect to R&D.[266] While some commentators wish to see a pan-European BDA,[267] others believe that substantive differences between the U.S. and Europe would render a European BDA ineffective.[268] Thomas Siepmann notes substantive differences between the U.S. and European university systems, notably that European researchers are not as interested in the exploitation of their research in the private sector.[269] Also notable is the difficulty in harmonizing the technology transfer sys-

263 *See* Mireles, *supra* note 75 , at 273. For an analysis of major differences in the university structure of the United States versus other countries, see Chapter I, *supra.*

264 *See* J. Steven Rutt and Stephen B. Maebium, *Technology Transfer Under Japan's Bayh-Dole: Boom or Bust Nanotechnology Opportunities?* 1 Nanotechnology Law and Business (Issue 3, Art. 8), at page 9. Though benefits of this scheme are yet to be conclusively studied, the shift in technology transfer from the former scheme of Government to industry (which focused on a very small number of companies) has much potential for success.

265 *See* Mireles, *supra* note 75, at 260.

266 *CEU Report on Research and Development*, at 42-46, CEU 5402/1/02 REV 1, (22 January, 2002) **A81** While the CEU falls short of stating that a Bayh-Dole Act should be passed throughout the EU, it seems to recommend similar actions to be taken to increase research and development across the union. Specifically, "the appropriate framework conditions" should be in place, and the "effectiveness of public research" should be improved. *See id* at pages 42 and 46.

267 *See* University Inventions – Europe Needs a Bayh-Dole Act, http://www.ipeg.eu/?p=1567 (August 7th, 2010). The writers note that "stronger protection for the results of publicly funded R&D would accelerate their commercialization and the realization of these economic benefits." The authors note that a full European Bayh-Dole Act would better encourage "more effective exploitation of university inventions.".

268 *See* Thomas J. Siepmann, *The Global Exportation of the U.S. Bayh-Dole Act,* 30 Dayton L. Rev 209, at 218 (2004).

269 *See id.* Other differences between the systems are noted in Chapter I-B, *supra.*

tem of multiple countries, which would be necessary if a full European BDA was announced.[270]

Irrespective of the concerns inherent in creating a full European Bayh-Dole Act, numerous countries have created Bayh-Dole-like legislation, and the effects of the legislation remain to be seen. For example, Germany enacted an amendment in 2002 which states that a university "now can lay claim to inventions created by its employees with government funding on its campus."[271] This amendment includes distinct stipulations regarding how much of the profits should go to specific employees, which may prove to resolve some issues that the U.S. Bayh-Dole Act leaves open.[272] While it will take decades to see the effect of the German amendment, the Max Planck Society technology transfer division has noted an increasing demand "from young scientists who want to start their own companies."[273] This could lead to the increase in collaboration and a growth in startups that would mirror the successes in the United States.

C. Bayh-Dole in Developing Countries? The Indian Bayh-Dole Debate

While Bayh-Dole has its critics, few can disagree with the contention that the United States university technology transfer industry has exploded in the last quarter-century, to which Bayh-Dole is at least partially responsible. The aforementioned research points in the direction of at least moderate success for technology transfer in developed countries. What remains to be seen, however, is if Bayh-Dole could have a beneficial effect in developing countries where the university system is much less structured, or if Bayh-Dole provisions may actually be detrimental for these countries.

India has been arguing about the merits of a BDA for years. The Utilisation of Public Funded Intellectual Property Bill 2008 is still being considered by the parliament, and includes protection and utilization requirements for publicly funded inventions.[274] This would effectively allow the Indian contractors to commercialize

270 *See generally id.* at 219. Siepmann also notes prohibitive costs in patent protection, and weak intellectual property laws in some EU countries would further inhibit the possibility of a true EU Bayh-Dole Act.

271 *Id.* at 222.

272 For example, employees must receive 30% of the profits stemming from commercialization. *See id.* Though this doesn't by any means preclude universities from needing to contract with employees for ownership rights, the rigid rule granting profits to an inventor may make an employee less likely to attempt to contract with an outside company, thus limiting the prevalence of a *Stanford v Roche*-type ownership problem.

273 *Id.*

274 *See* Rahul Vartak and Manish Saurastri, *The Indian Version of the Bayh-Dole Act,* INTELLECTUAL ASSET MANAGEMENT, March/April 2009, at 62, *hereinafter* "Indian Bayh-Dole.".

their research and patent their inventions, which is not possible under the current scheme.[275]

The bill's supporters consider the act an improvement as it provides greater clarity on title, and an interface between funding agencies, academia, and industry.[276] Proponents note the success of Bayh-Dole in the U.S., and believe this "copycat" bill will lead to similar results. However, the bill's critics see fundamental differences between the U.S. and India, and maintain that the "hastily drafted" copycat bill does not take into account the complexities of the Indian technology transfer industry.[277]

The Indian Bayh-Dole proposal has been attacked in two ways. Some note the shortfalls of the U.S. BDA and decide that it would be unhelpful to bring similar problems to India. The second school of thought acknowledges successes of the U.S. BDA, but that India's technology transfer is a "serious disconnect" from the United States and transplantation of an American statute would fail.[278]

1. Shortfalls of the United States Bayh-Dole Act

Annette Lin et al. criticize the Indian Bayh-Dole bill by alluding to assumed failures of the United States BDA.[279] The authors see the U.S. BDA as too narrowly focused on patenting and licensing, while failing to recognize publishing, teaching, and other collaboration.[280] They further state that U.S. BDA has not generated consistent revenues, noting that profitability numbers have been skewed by several "blockbuster" inventions for some universities, while others fail to profit whatsoever.[281] The authors also echo many American critics who feel that the Bayh-Dole model and its increased incentive to patent early will threaten access to life-saving drugs.[282] With India's large generic drugs international market, a Bayh-Dole bill may effectively harm consumers worldwide. The authors finally fear that the Bayh-Dole scheme may have a "chilling effect" on the exchange of knowledge, because financial gain has replaced "recognition and esteem" as the basic tenet that re-

275 *See* Indian Bayh-Dole, *supra* note 274. The scheme in India is similar to the United States pre-Bayh Dole scheme with respect to Government title of publicly funded inventions.

276 *See id.*

277 *See id.*

278 *See* Shamnad Basheer and Shouvik Guha, OUTSOURCING BAYH-DOLE TO INDIA: LOST IN TRANSPLANTATION? 270 *available at* http://ssrn.com/abstract=1546403.

279 *See* Annette Lin et al., *The Bayh-Dole Act and Promoting the Transfer of Technology of Publicly Funded-Research* Universities Allied for Essential Medicines, *available at* http://essentialmedicine.org/sites/default/files/archive/uaem-white-paper-on-indian-bd-act.pdf.

280 *See id.* The authors feel that broader focus would better achieve the objectives and needs of India.

281 *See id.*

282 *See id.*

searchers follow, and inherent in this is added secrecy and potential withholding of knowledge.[283]

2. Differences between India and the United States

Shamnad Basheer and Shouvik Guha attack the bill on the grounds that success in the United States would not necessarily lead to success in India.[284] The authors contend that legal transplantation is "often unsuccessful if external forces, such as international institutions, assume institutional, cultural, or political realities that in fact are not present or properly developed."[285]

The authors note that aspiration of the Bill is to "create wealth." Basheer and Gupta agree with the contention of Lin et al. that legislators have exaggerated the United States Bayh-Dole bill's success in this regard, but further extend their analysis by considering particular aspects in the Indian market that could lead to a Bayh-Dole failure. For example, the Council of Scientific and Industrial Research in India (CSIR) is actually losing money on its patents, which is evidence pointing to the conclusion that Bayh-Dole provisions would have a very limited effect.[286]

The authors further attack specific provisions of the bill as unable to effectively promote technology transfer. For example, the proposal "assumes that patents are always the best way to incentivize innovation and requires patent application in all cases."[287] In India, the cost of patents are prohibitive at times, and the inability to make an ex ante determination of what inventions will benefit from patents will unduly inhibit effective transfer under the Indian scheme.[288]

The authors ultimately conclude that for a bill like Bayh-Dole to be effective in India, it should include "more public interest safeguards," and an "affordable pricing scheme," among other changes.[289] While Basheer and Lin et al. differ on reasons that the Indian Bayh-Dole Bill would be a concern if passed, they agree that the United States BDA would not be beneficial if superimposed on India without much

283 *See id.*

284 *See* Basheer and Guha, *supra* note 278.

285 *Id.* at 278. The others define legal transplantation as "the transfer of laws and institutional structures across geopolitical or cultural borders." *See id* at 277.

286 *See id.* at 282. The CSIR is a "network of government laboratories" and one of India's largest patent filers. By noting that this government organization is not profiting off patents it has title to, the authors believe that shifting the title to universities will lead to the same result as CSIR has attempted to commercialize its patents just as a university would.

287 *Id.* at 284.

288 *See id.* at 285.

289 *Id.* at 298-300. The affordable pricing scheme would be similar to what some American scholars believe is inherent in the US Bayh-Dole Act, and others believe do not exist at all. For more on this question, please see Section *V-A-4*, *supra*.

thought. The concerns in India might mirror concerns in other developing countries with respect to using Bayh-Dole schemes.

VII. Conclusion

While it is relatively undisputed that the BDA fostered uniformity among federal agencies, which led to more licensing by universities and less uncertainty with respect to ownership, the ultimate effect on technology transfer is not unanimously agreed upon.[290] Though the number of patents to universities has increased drastically since the passing of the Act, some Bayh-Dole detractors contend that the BDA was an effect, not the cause, of the explosion in innovation. However, the Act has empirically been shown to have improved the technology transfer of federally funded university inventions, with commercialization and licensing of patents increasing substantially post-1980. Further, it seems clear that the BDA has neither hampered scientific progress nor misdirected research any more than what would occur in a regulation-free system. The major concern of many critics is the possibility of an anticommons effect pursuant to the increase in early stage patenting. Evidence of commercialization shows that, to this point, an anticommons has not occurred.

Despite the successes of the statute, the provision for the march-in by the government in specific cases has proved to be a failure. The government has never marched in and asserted its power, and the statute needs to be reworked to incentivize the government to do so when the situation is warranted. The options that can instigate a march-in have merit; the hesitance of the government to use these options needs change. Explicitly defining examples that should lead to march-in and including a reasonable pricing requirement will make the march-in provision more effective as both a deterrent and a tool to ensure commercialization occurs.

The *Stanford* case has given rise to a previously unexamined limitation of Bayh-Dole—specifically the fact that the Act does not automatically override the rights given to an inventor under patent law. Thus, universities will have to be more vigilant in ensuring that inventors contract their rights in patent to the university. Further, the increased likelihood that a commercial invention will have multiple owners of patents forming the invention may create an anticommons effect, and thus faintly harm the technology transfer system. Despite these consequences, the case was correctly decided from a policy standpoint. If Bayh-Dole were to be interpreted to override patent law principles, the effect on technology transfer would prove to be more harmful, as individual researchers will be even less incentivized to work towards creating patentable products.

290 *See* Managing University Intellectual Property in the Public Interest 1 (Stephen A. Merrill and Anne-Marie Mazza eds., The National Academy Press) 2011.

Though the BDA has proved worthwhile in the United States, great care must be taken to create similar statutes abroad. The differences between the United States university system and those in other countries are substantial, and must be considered when creating a provision to allow for universities to keep rights to their patents. India is a classic case where a country has acknowledged differences between itself and the United States, and the result is a bill that has been under construction for several years. To increase the chances of progression in its university technology transfer sector, a country must narrowly tailor any regulations to account for the university structure, commercialization tendencies, and cultural makeup. While time will be the ultimate judge of the effect of "Bayh-Dole-esque" provisions, studies and analysis of Bayh-Dole in the United States and the similarities and differences of technology transfer in the relevant country will maximize the opportunities for improvement in university technology transfer.

Appendix A

Patents Issued to U.S. Research Universities (1925-1995)

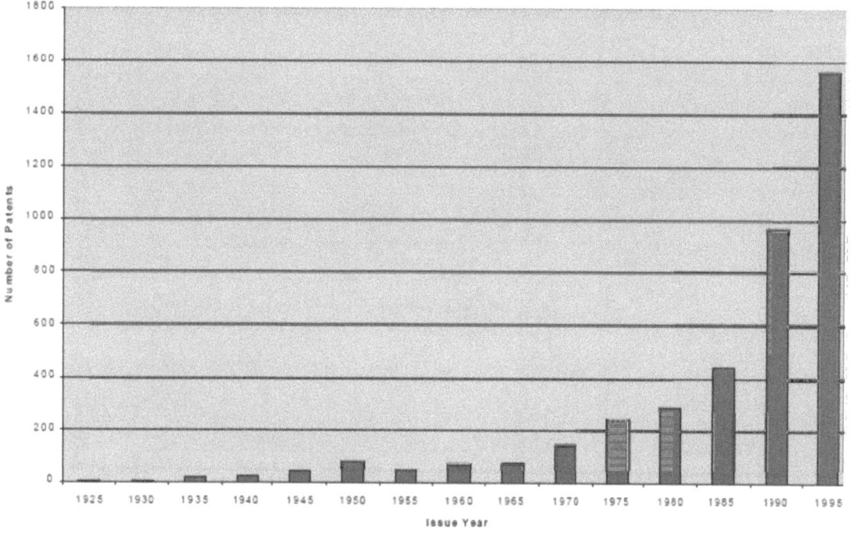

List of Works Cited

Cases

Ass'n for Molecular Pathology et al. v. United States Patent and Trademark Office et al., 702 F. Supp 2d 181 (S.D.N.Y. 2010), rev'd in part, 2011 U.S. App. Lexis 15649 (Fed. Cir, 2011).

Board of Trustees of the Leland Stanford Junior University v Roche Molecular Systems, Inc., et al., 563 U. S.___ (2011)

Board of Trustees of the Leland Stanford Junior University v. Roche Molecular Systems, Inc. 583 F.3d 832 (Fed. Cir, 2008), aff'd 563 U.S. ____ (2011)

Campbell Plastics Eng. v. Brownlee, 389 F.3d 1243, 1250 (Fed. Cir. 2004)

Damond v. Chakrabarty, 447 U.S. 303 (1979).

Fenn v. Yale Univ., 393 F. Supp. 2d 133, 141-4 (D. Conn. 2004)

Filmtec Corporation v. Allied-Signal Inc., 939 F.2d 1568, 1572 (Fed. Cir. 1991)

Univ. of Rochester v. G.D. Searle & Co., 358 F.3d 916, 929 (Fed. Cir, 2004)

Statutes and Regulations

37 C.F.R. § 401.3(b) (2004)

37 C.F.R. § 401.6 (2006).

FAR 27.302(b)(2)

15 U.S.C.A. § 3701 (2011)

35 U.S.C. §§ 101-103 (2008)

35 U.S.C. § 112 (2008)

35 U.S.C. §§ 200-203 (2009)

35 U.S.C. § 210 (2009)

Legislative Reports and Materials

GAO REP. NO. 09-742, at 10-11, *reprinted at* http://www.gao.gov/htext/d09742html

H.R. CON. RES. 319, 109th Cong. (2005), at 2, *reprinted in* H.R. REP. NO. 109-409

Journal Articles

Arno, Peter and *Davis, Michael*: Why Don't We Enforce Existing Drug Price Controls? The Unrecognized and Unenforced Reasonable Pricing Requirements Imposed upon Patents Deriving in Whole or in Part from Federally Funded Research, 75 TULANE L. REV. 631, (2001)

Boumil, Marcia and *Berman, Harris:* Revisiting the Physician/Industry Alliance: The Bayh-Dole Act and Conflict of Interest Management at Academic Medical Centers. 15 MICH. STATE UNIV. OF Medicine & Law 1 (2010)

Bremer, Howard et al.: The Bayh-Dole Act and Revisionism Redux, at page 6, Life Sciences Law & Industry, Vol. 3, No. 17 (September 11, 2009)

Eberle, Mary: March-In Rights Under the Bayh-Dole Act: Public Access to Federally Funded Research, 3 MARQ. INTELL. PROP. L. REV. 155 (1999)

Eisenberg, Rebecca: Symposium on Regulating Medical Innovation: Public Research and Private Development: Patents and Technology Transfer in Government-Sponsored Research, 82 VA. L. REV. 1663 (1996)

Hamilton, Clovia: University Technology Transfer and Economic Development: Proposed Cooperative Economic Development Agreements Under the Bayh-Dole Act, 36 J. MARSHALL L. REV. 397 (2003)

Heller, Michael and *Eisenberg, Rebecca*: Can Patents Deter Innovation? The Anticommons in Biomedical Research, Science, Vol. 280, 1 May 1998

Lowe, Robert A.: Who Develops a University Invention? The Impact of Tacit Knowledge and Licensing Policies, 31 J. TECH. TRANSFER (Netherlands) 415 (2006)

McCabe, Kevin: Implications of the CellPro Deteermination on Inventions Made with Federal Assistance: Will the Government Ever Exercise its March-In Right? 27 PUB. CONT. L.J. 645 (1998)

McGarey, Barbara & Levey, Annette: Patents, Products, and Public Health: An Analysis of the CellPro March-in Petition, 14 BERKLEY TECH L.J. 1095 (1999)

Mireles, Michael: Adoption of the Bayh-Dole Act in Developed Countries: Added Pressure for a Broad Research Exemption in the United States?, 59 ME. L. REV. 259 (2007).

Moore, Chester G.: Killing the Bayh-Dole Act's Golden Goose, 8 TUL. L. J. TECH. & INTELL. PROP. 151, (2006)

Mowery, David et al.: The growth of patenting and licensing by U.S. universities: an assessment of the effects of the Bayh-Dole act of 1980, 30 RES. POL. (ELSEVIER) 99, (2001)

Namikawa, Ryoichi: Intellectual property in R&D project under Japanese Bayh-Dole system, 9-1/2 Int. J. Technology Transfer and Commercialisation 9 (2010)

Richard R. Nelson, Observations on the Post-Bayh-Dole Rise of Patenting at American Universities, 26 J. TECH. TRANSFER 13 (2001)

Pulsinelli, Gary: Share and Share Alike: Increasing Access to Government-Funded Inventions Under the Bayh-Dole Act, 7 MINN J.L. SCI. & TECH 393 (2006)

Rai, Arti and *Eisenberg, Rebecca*: The Public Domain: Bayh-Dole Reform and the Progress and Biomedicine, 66 LAW AND CONTEMP. PROBS. 289 (2003).

Raubitschek, John and *Latker, Norman:* Reasonable Pricing – A New Twist for March-In Rights Under the Bayh-Dole Act, 22 SANTA CLARA COMPUTER & HIGH TECH L.J. 149 (2005)

Ream, Rachel: Nonprofit Commercialization Under Bayh-Dole and the Academic Anti-commons, 58 CASE W. RES. L. REV. 1343 (2008)

Rutt, Steven and Maebium, Stephen: Technology Transfer Under Japan's Bayh-Dole: Boom or Bust Nanotechnology Opportunities? 1 Nanotechnology Law and Business (Issue 3, Art. 8)

Rutt, Steven: Federal Government Clarifies "March-In" Rights Under Bayh-Dole System, *available at* http://www.nanocleantechblog.com/2010/04/articles/legislation/federal-government-clarifies marchin-rights-under-bayhdole-system/ (April 23, 2010).

Sharma, Sanjesh: The Bayh-Dole Act and Allocation of Ownership Rights in Inventions Arising out of Federally Funded Research, 8 INTELL. PROP. & TECH. L.J. 23 (August, 2011)

Siepmann, Thomas: The Global Exportation of the U.S. Bayh-Dole Act, 30 DAYTON L. REV 209, at 218 (2004).

Vartak, Rahul and *Saurastri, Manish:* The Indian Version of the Bayh-Dole Act, INTELLECTUAL ASSET MANAGEMENT, March/April 2009

Books and Compilations

Graham, Hugh Davis and *Diamond* Nancy: THE RISE OF AMERICAN RESEARCH UNIVERSITIES, (Baltimore: Johns Hopkins University Press 1997).

MANAGING UNIVERSITY INTELLECTUAL PROPERTY IN THE PUBLIC INTEREST 1 (Stephen A. Merrill and Anne-Marie Mazza eds., The National Academy Press) 2011.

Mowery, David et al.: IVORY TOWER AND INDUSTRIAL INNOVATION: UNIVERSITY-INDUSTRY TECHNOLOGY TRANSFER BEFORE AND AFTER THE BAYH-DOLE ACT IN THE UNITED STATES 97 (Martin Kenney and Bruce Kogut eds., Stanford University Press) (2004)

Nash, Ralph and *Rawicz, Leonard*: INTELLECTUAL PROPERTY IN GOVERNMENT CONTRACTS 238 (The George Washington University 6 ed.) (2008)

Non-Journal Articles and Other Supplementary Materials with Author Explicit (alphabetical by author)

Barnes, Robert: Supreme Court limits patent rights of university research, WASH. POST, June 7, 2011, *available at* http://www.washingtonpost.com/politics/supreme-court-limits-patentrights-of university-research/2011/06/06/AG0UpbKH_story.html

Basheer, Shamnad and Guha, Shouvik: OUTSOURCING BAYH-DOLE TO INDIA: LOST IN TRANSPLANTATION? 270 *available at* http://ssrn.com/abstract=1546403

Berks, Andrew: Stanford v. Roche – When is an assignment not an assignment?, http://berksiplaw.com/2011/06/stanford-v-roche/ (June 12, 2011)

Buenstorf, Guido and Geissler, Matthias: Not invented here: Technology licensing, knowledge transfer and innovation based on public research, Papers on Economics and Evolution, Max-Planck-Gesellschaft (December, 2009).

Burrone, Esteban: Patents at the Core: the Biotech Business, World Intellectual Property Office, available at http://www.wipo.int/sme/en/documents/patents_biotech.htm

Carik, Joseph et al.: "PETITION TO USE AUTHORITY UNDER THE BAYH-DOLE ACT TO PROMOTE ACCESS TO FABRYZYME (AGALSIDASE BETA), AN INVENTION SUPPORTED BY AND LICENSED BY THE NATIONAL INSTITUTES OF HEALTH UNDER GRANT NO. DK-34045, *available at* http://www.genomicslawreport.com/wp content/uploads/2011/01/Fabrazyme-Bayh-Dole-Petition.pdf

Cain, Jonathan T. et al.: Invention Assignment Following *Stanford v. Roche:* Implications for TechnologyTransfer and Government Contracts, *published by* LexisNexis Martindale-Hubbell, June 30, 2011

Conley, John: Government Refused to March-In Under Bayh-Dole – Again, Genomics Law Report, January 8, 2011, *available at* http://www.genomicslawreport.com/index.php/2011/01/18/government-refuses-to-march-in-under-bayh-dole-again/

Gifford, Ernest I. Who's the owner?, Michigan Bar Journal 21-23 (Aug, 2004).

Halperin, David: The Bayh-Dole Act and March-in Rights, May 2001, prepared at the request of Consumer Project on Technology, *available at* http://www.ott.nih.gov/policy/meeting/David Halperin-Attorney-Counselor.pdf

Henderson, Jennifer and Smith, John: Academia, Industry, and the Bayh-Dole Act: An Implied Duty to Commercialize, *paper supported in part by* a grant from the Center for Integration of Medicine and Innovative Technology (CIMIT)

James, Kathryn: The *Myriad* decision: Judicial criticism of the Bayh-Dole Act and its progeny?, ABA Health eSource Vol 6-10 (June 2010)

Kettner, David and *Decker, William*: Fundamentals of Technology Transfer and Intellectual Property Licensing, November 2004 NACUA CLE Workshop Outline, *reprinted in* Technology Transfer Issues for Colleges and Universities: A Legal Compendium (Judith L. Curry, ed., National Association of College and University Attorneys (NACUA) 2005)

Lin, Annette et al.: The Bayh-Dole Act and Promoting the Transfer of Tecnology of Publicly Funded-Research, Universities Allied for Essential Medicines, *available at* http://essentialmedicine.org/sites/default/files/archive/uaem-white-paper-on-indian-bd-act.pdf

Loise, Vickey and Stevens, Ashley: The Bayh-Dole Act Turns 30, les Nouvelles 185, at 190 (December 2010)

McManis, Charles and *Noh, Sucheol*: THE IMPACT OF THE BAYH-DOLE ACT ON GENETIC RESEARCH AND DEVELOPMENT: EVALUATING THE ARGUMENTS AND EMPIRICAL EVIDENCE TO DATE 13, *available at* papers.ssrn.com/sol3/papers.cfm?abstract_id=1840639

Mendes, Phillip: To License a Patent – or, to Assign it: Factors Influencing the Choice, *published by* WIPO, *available at* http://wipo.int/export/sites/www/sme/en/documents/pdf/license_assign_patent.pdf.

Mowery, David and Sampat, Bhaven: University Patents and Policy Debates: 1925-1980, prepared for Conference at Columbia University, October 13-15, 2000. *Available at professor murmann.net/nelsonfest/moweryp.doc*

Philippidis, Alex: Stanford v. Roche Could Place Tech Transfer on Shaky Ground, Genetic Engineering & Biotechnology News, Mar 17, 2011, *available at* http://www.genengnews.com/analysis-and-insight/i-stanford-v-roche-i-could-place-tech-transfer on-shaky-ground/77899372/

Roessner David et al.: The Economic Impact of Licensed Commercialized Inventions Originating in University Research, *1996-200,* Final Report to the Biotechnology Industry Organization (September 3, 2009)

Wahlberg, David: Emory Gets $525 Million Payment for Emtriva, Atl. J. Const., July 19, 2005, *quoted in* HIVPlusmag.com, *available* at http://www.hivplusmag.com/NewsStory.asp?id=12287&sd=07/20/2005

Articles and Other Supplementary Materials without Explicit Author (alphabetical by title)

Bayh-Dole Act, UD Research, University of Delaware, available at *http://www.udel.edu/research/protecting/bayh-dole.html*

The Bayh-Dole Act at 25: BayhDole25, Inc., April 17, 2006

CEU Report on Research and Development, at 42-46, CEU 5402/1/02 REV 1, (22 January, 2002)

Determination in the Case of Fabrazyme (Nat'l Inst. Of Health, 2010) at 1, *hereinafter* "NIH-Fabrazyme", *available at* http://www.ott.nih.gov/policy/March-in-Fabrazyme.pdf

Determination in the Case of Petition of CellPro, Inc. (Nat'l Inst. Of Health, 1997) at 3, *hereinafter* "NIH-CellPro", *available at* http://www.nih.gov/news/pr/aug97/nihb-01.htm

The Fair Rewards of Invention, N.Y. Times, June 7, 2011 (Op-Ed), *reprinted a* http://www.nytimes.com/2011/06/08/opinion/08wed3.html?_r=1

Gilead Sciences and Royalty Pharma Announce $525 Million Agreement with Emory University to Purchase Royalty Interest for Emtricitabine (July 18, 2005), Press Release, Gilead Sciences, Emory University and Royalty Pharma, (*available at* http://www.emory.edu/news/Releases/emtri)

Innovation's golden goose: The reforms that unleashed American innovation in the 1980s, and were emulated widely around the world, are under attack at home, The Economist, Dec 12, 2002

Model License Agreement: Exclusive License Agreement Between The Johns Hopkins University & ____, reprinted in Technology Transfer Issues for Colleges and Universities: A Legal Compendium (Judith L. Curry, ed., National Association of College and University Attorneys (NACUA) 2005) at 265

Patent and Copyright Agreement for Stanford Personnel, Research Policy Handbook: Memo, *available at* http://rph.stanford.edu/su18.html

Patent policy flaws complicate commercialization of federally funded university discoveries, News Release, Duke University (December 11, 2002) (*available at* http://www.eurekaalert.org/pub_releases/2002-12/du-ppfl120602.php

Research Policies: University of Delaware Office of the Executive Vice President and University Treasurer, *available at* http://www.udel.edu/ExecVP/policies/research/6-06.html

Stanford v. Roche, Bayh-Dole and the Intersection of Patent and Tax Exemption, Nonprofit Law Prof Blog, http://lawprofessors.typepad.com/nonprofit/2011/06/stanford-v-roche-bayh-dole-and-the-intersection-of-patent-and-tax-exemption.html (June 21, 2011).

Stanford v. Roche decision requires extra care in managing university IP, The Tech Transfer Blog, http://www.technologytransfertactics.com/content/2011/07/13/stanford-v-roche-decision-requires extra-care-in-managing-university-ip/ (July 13, 2011)

Supreme Court to hear Bayh-Dole Patent Ownership Dispute: Stanford v. Roche, Patently-O: The nation's leading patent law blog, *available at* http://www.patentlyo.com/patent/2010/11/supreme court-to-hear-bayh-dole-patent-ownership- dispute-stanford-v-roche.html (Nov 01, 2010)

University Inventions – Europe Needs a Bayh-Dole Act, http://www.ipeg.eu/?p=1567 (August 7th, 2010)

What is the Bayh-Dole Act, What Prompted it, and Why is it important to University Technology Transfer? University of Hawaii, Office of Technology and Transfer and Economic Development, *available at* http://www.otted.hawaii.edu/what-bayh-dole-act

Zeitfracht Medien GmbH
Ferdinand-Jühlke-Straße 7
99095 Erfurt, Deutschland
produktsicherheit@kolibri360.de